# Aisles for Miles

## my years as a nuptial concierge/wedding doula

## by Natalie M. Stahl

### Jody Serey, Editor

SEREYJONES
PUBLISHERS

The events and conversations in this book have been set down to the best of the
author's ability, although some names and details have been changed or omitted to
protect the privacy of individuals.

Cover photo by Natalie M. Stahl
Back cover photo by Joanna Roe Photography

Published in the United States by
Serey/Jones Publishers, Inc.
www.sereyjones.com

ISBN:  978-1-881276-23-4  (paperback)
10ww

# Table of Contents

## Virginia's House

## Family, Friends, People

# Vendors

# Angels Among Us

# Conclusion

# Virginia's House

## Million dollar baby

I didn't mean to own a wedding venue. Don't get me wrong, the act was deliberate – I just never thought it would be a reality. When my husband and I were first married, it was the what-would-you-do-if-you-won-a-million-dollars discussion. It sounded like fun – get invited to parties. Work the weekends. Make a lot of money with our investment. I just never thought it would be a possibility – you know, winning the lottery and everything.

I worked for a large corporation as the grocery buyer for a convenience store chain. Not real glamorous, but I was good at it and I liked it – for a job. We had been married for two years when our first daughter was born. My pregnancy was a difficult one with several scares along the way. Our baby girl was born a little over a month early via emergency C-section.

Everyone says the day your baby is born changes your life. It did. But nothing prepared me for the day that I handed her over to someone else one morning and headed back to work. THAT is the day that changed my life. I realized then that I had won something far greater than a million dollars. I was entrusted with this tiny little baby's life.

My husband and I had been to a wedding the weekend before I went back to work. Ironically enough, it was his ex-girl-friend's wedding (it's okay – really). I was being a little catty that night. The DJ was particularly annoying about "watching your step around the pool". And I was a little more opinion-ated than usual about trivial things – the punch bowl, the room the food was in, etc. (Hey – cut me some slack. I was at the ex's wedding…). My husband uttered those fateful words, "If you think you can do better, why don't you?"

Dumb move, dude. I'm the type of girl to take that as a per-sonal challenge. A dare. Game on.

# Take the long way home

One of the things that my husband and I love to do is take the long way home. This usually means driving through an old neighborhood we've never seen before or taking a different route. We both share a love for old houses and quirky neighborhoods.

This night, after the wedding, we took the long way home. We were weaving through old neighborhoods in Glendale when we passed a large white house on a corner. It had a "for sale" sign in the yard. I tapped my husband on the arm, pointed at the house and said, "There's my wedding house."

He chuckled. I said, "No. It is. The hair on my arm just stood up. I know it is."

He thinks I'm a little nutty, anyway. I'm sure that was just part of my initial "mystery" or "intrigue" when we first met. But I remembered the phone number from the sign and called it when I got to work on Monday. It was for sale. It was old. And it was barely in range to afford it. So of course, I scheduled an appointment to view it.

# We'll take it

We met the realtor later that week. When we first entered the house, I was disappointed. The rooms were small and choppy and didn't make much sense. But we were there, so we continued the tour. We wandered through the maze of rooms that were painted all shades of Easter egg colors.

We got to the end of a hallway with a door. My husband was looking into a small room when I turned the knob of the door. When I pushed open that door, I nearly fainted. The living room had high ceilings that soared to eleven feet and was one of the biggest rooms I had seen. We both just stood there in awe. As we wandered into the dining room, parlor, butler's pantry and kitchen – it just got better and better. There were plate ledges, picture rails and even a window seat. My heart bought the house at that very moment.

# Real estate and other mysterious things

We went scurrying about with flashes of paperwork – offers, contracts, contingencies, dreaming. We signed a contract for six months. If we could sell our current house, the lovely old home would be ours.

Those six months ticked by and came to a close with nearly no activity on the sale of our current home. On my way home from work on the final day, I resolved myself to believe that there was something better coming and I would graciously let this one go. The timing probably wasn't right anyway – having a brand-new baby, and all.

Our realtor called that night and insisted on coming over. We told him on the phone that we weren't interested in extending the contract. He insisted on coming anyway.

When he got there, he was grinning from ear to ear. He said, "What would you think about a cash offer for full asking price?" We were stunned, speechless and obviously said "yes".

# So here we are – now what?

So, we bought an 80-something-year-old house. We were both 30 years old and had a six-month-old baby. What we didn't have was a plan.

We jumped in and started painting, scraping and indulged in general renovation madness. This went on for nearly two years. We had to add fencing, a gazebo, grass, flowers and pretty things.

Our baby learned how to walk in a construction zone and would hand us things like nails and hammers and say, "No, no, baby." Thankfully she policed herself. (She would often start wailing and crying, "I wanna go to Depot." Poor kid. Home Depot was fun for her.)

# Standing in the aisle

So, there I was. A business owner with no business. Because this was 1998 before the internet and social media, customers were a lot harder to find. I took out ads in the local wedding magazines. I stood in the convention center for long weekends peddling my venue to unsuspecting brides at bridal (should read "brutal") shows.

One day, I was standing in the wedding aisle of a craft store. A bride and her mother were arguing about wedding-related things. At that moment in time, I swallowed every piece of pride and dignity that I ever possessed and butted into their conversation. I told them that I owned a new wedding venue in Glendale and I would love to show them around. Maybe I could help them come to wedding resolutions without so much fighting. And they said yes. They. Said. Yes.

As it turned out, they booked my venue. I rented furniture and hired a photographer. I needed to get photos of this event so I could use it in advertising and actually LOOK like I was in business.

November 7, 1998 Virginia's House hosted its first wedding and reception.

# Friday the 13th

I was on cloud nine. I actually felt like a legitimate business owner! I had pulled off my first event and I LOVED it!

What I didn't love was my "new" boss. Remember that corporate job? I still had it. My favorite boss had been transferred to a different department right after my daughter was born and I was struggling to find a groove with the new boss. The hours of my corporate job were hard to keep up with, particularly with renovation and a small child.

This particular week, the new boss was worse than he had ever been. On Thursday, he pulled me into his office and proceeded to chew me out for literally the entire afternoon. After about the first 10 minutes, I think he went on a repeated loop. I'm not sure. I stopped listening. As I sat there, I realized that I didn't want to drive for an hour each way to be abused by him when I got there. I had started down the path of my new vision and I needed to make a go of it.

My husband and I talked about it all night Thursday. Friday morning, I went to work and fired my boss. Or quit my job. Actually, I went to his boss – I was done being the object of my boss's diatribes. The marketing VP asked me to stay through the end of the year and said he would make sure I received my full bonus. I told him I would under one condition – that I reported directly to him. And not the miserable frat boy that hated me. It was a deal.

I was proud of myself, but scared to death. So, I called my old boss – the one I loved and my biggest fan. He yelled out loud when I told him what I had done. His words are burned into my brain. And I've had to refer back to them often. He said, "Run. Run fast. Don't ever look back."

That's exactly what I did.

*Run. Run fast. Don't ever look back.*

# History of the home

Cullen H. Tinker was a prominent banker in early Glendale, and later served the town as its third mayor from 1916 to 1922. He and wife Josie (nee Bramhall) had two children, Katherine and Josephine. He began his business career in Texas in 1897, and relocated his family to Glendale in 1911.

Upon his arrival in Arizona in 1911, Tinker purchased the Glendale State Bank. W. H. Slaughter had started the bank in 1909, and by 1912 it had assets of almost $50,000. Tinker built the bank up over the next four years until its assets reached $125,000.

In June of 1916, Tinker started his own bank in Glendale. The Security State Bank opened for business, and in its first year took in almost $150,000 in deposits. In 1917, Tinker acquired the Hotchkiss Building and remodeled it for his new bank. In 1918, the Security State Bank became the first Glendale bank to join the Federal Reserve System. Tinker then changed the name of the bank to First National Bank of Glendale.

At about this time, Tinker launched his political career. He was elected mayor in 1916, and was re-elected in 1918 and 1920, serving a total of three terms. His tenure in office was a time of remarkable growth and expansion in Glendale. In addition to his banking and political endeavors, Tinker contributed to Glendale's prosperity by heading up the Glendale Ice Company, which permitted railroad cars to ship produce packed in ice – a definite boon to the agriculturally-based local economy.

By 1924, Tinker's bank had survived many ups and downs, and boasted deposits of 500,000. He negotiated an agreement with the Valley Bank to merge institutions, and the resulting institution became known as Valley National Bank.

Tinker stayed on as Glendale branch manager for two years, and in 1926 became vice president of Valley Bank's Phoenix branch. In 1931, be became vice-president of the Valley Bank itself, until he was forced to resign in 1943 for reasons of poor health.

Construction of the C.H. Tinker House is associated with the development of Glendale outside of the original townsite. In 1913, C.H. Tinker completed construction of his residence. The house was designed by J.R. Kibbey of the noted architectural firm of Lescher and Kibbey as a comparatively small neo-classical revival-style bungalow. In 1919, Kibbey remodeled extensively.

In 1936, Tinker sold the house to Alph and Dorothy May Jorgenson. Alph Jorgenson managed the J.C. Penney store in Glendale through the Depression and until after World War II. The location of the Tinker House, on the west side of Glendale on a major thoroughfare to Luke Field, made it a particularly attractive spot for renters.

The Tinker House was known to military personnel and defense plant workers as the "Jorgenson Apartments." One of the renters was John J. Hook, who with his wife Virginia eventually purchased the property from the Jorgensen family. Mrs. Hook gradually returned the property to a one-family dwelling, and the C. H. Tinker House became a "home" once again.

On February 28, 1997 Scott and Natalie M. Stahl acquired the Tinker House from the Hook family. Since that time, they have lovingly restored the old home to its 1919 appearance. The couple renamed the property "Virginia's House" to honor long-time owner Virginia Hook, who lived in the house for almost 50 years. The house has been featured on the Home & Garden Television Channel's program, "Restore America."

# What's in a name?

When we purchased the property, it was my wish to be able to name the business after something historic that we had learned. Because the house's history is relatively short, I was coming up short with what to call it.

As you read in the historic narrative of the home, we purchased the home from Virginia Hook in 1997. Her husband, John, had died a couple of years earlier. Truth be told, she wasn't ready to leave her beloved home. It had been her point of pride for decades and it broke her heart to leave it. But as it was, she was having a hard time keeping up with it. And her family was having a hard time, as well.

She spent her last Christmas here in 1996. Christmas was one of her great loves. She loved decorating for the holiday and having guests. All of the pictures she showed me were taken at Christmastime.

Christmas 1997 was our first Christmas here. Our daughter had just turned one and we were headlong into renovating the property. The house is located in downtown Glendale, one block from the town square. Glendale is known for its millions of Christmas lights in the park.

On the first night of the annual park lighting, we had the baby in the stroller and were heading to the park. The traffic light was about to change and there was an older woman struggling to cross the street with her walker. I handed the baby off to my husband and went to help her move along.

I learned that her name was Olive and that she had lived in Glendale her entire life. She asked where we were coming from. I told her that we had recently purchased a historic home and gestured towards the house. She said, "My dearest friend Virginia used to live over there."

I said, "WE bought Virginia's house!" And there it was – my business name. All of the ladies in town knew my beautiful old house to be Virginia's.

I was quick to call Mrs. Hook the next day and ask her permission to use her name. She very politely declined saying that we didn't have to do that. When I told her I WANTED to, she said that she loved the idea. And so it was.

Virginia's House got registered with the state in June that same year. I made sure that Mrs. Hook got a copy of every magazine that I ran an ad in. Rumor has it that she carried those magazines around her retirement complex and showed everyone. I love that.

I kept in touch with Mrs. Hook for years. When my kids were babies, we often went for visits. Because Christmas was a big deal for her, we always took her a Christmas gift – usually a small ornament.

She returned to her previous home one time – actually twice. Once to plan her final Christmas party, then the actual party itself. I was very humbled to be able to host that party for her. It was at least 8 years after she had moved out – possibly longer – that she came back. She said it was very hard for her to return. She had a perfectly formed memory of her house and she didn't want that memory replaced.

As she got older, I was worried that she would pass away without me knowing it, but we were connected through enough people. When she was placed in hospice, I was notified immediately. She had suffered a stroke and never regained consciousness.

When I walked into her funeral, I was met by her son, daughter-in-law and grandchildren. The first words out of her daughter-in-law was, "I knew you would be here." And I was. I still miss her. She was 96 years old.

Christmas continues to be a very special time at Virginia's House. I think she would love it. I have a stack of Christmas cards that she sent me every year. I am thankful to be able to carry on her love of Christmas here. And her love of love. We've got that, too.

# Family, Friends, People

## Sometimes it's hard for adults to act like adults

It's true. Sometimes we put too much faith in the belief that adults will act like adults. We don't take into consideration heartbreaks, family fights, or general personality disorders.

We had a gorgeous bride and a doting groom. It was a wintertime wedding with sparkly things everywhere. The bride was wrapped in a beautiful faux fur shrug and looked like a million bucks. Her groom couldn't keep his eyes off his beautiful bride. The photographer was trying to capture all this love and beauty to be cherished forever by setting up a family picture.

13

It was a medium-sized group and the photographer was doing her level best to get everyone in the frame. She moved and adjusted and got everyone where they needed to be. She then invited the groom's dad to remove his Blu-Blocker sunglasses and his Bluetooth for the picture. He said no. Then the bride (very gently) asked him please remove it just for the picture. That's when the earth cracked...

The groom's dad called the bride some very inappropriate and somewhat colorful names because of her request. The groom quickly told his father not to speak to his wife that way. And almost immediately, the groomsmen grabbed him by his hair and dragged him to the gate.

*Wedding days should be off-limits for outbursts. If you can't act like an adult, get a babysitter.*

My staff and the couple's guests were stunned for what seemed like a few minutes, but I'm sure it was only seconds. As the venue owner, I was glad that someone else was taking care of removing him – I didn't want to worry about him for the rest of the evening. But one of my staff members – having a cooler head than mine – followed them out and removed the groomsmen from his neck. She explained life to him as best as she could and asked him to rethink his departure. She also put him on notice that if he acted up again that the police would be his next escort off the property.

(Side note – his Bluetooth had dialed my desk phone in the melee and my voice mail had recorded the entire incident.)

The groom's dad sat very quietly and obediently at his table for the rest of the evening. Not sure if he was embarrassed or scared. Either way – he wasn't invited into any more photos and I don't believe he danced with the bride.

Note to self: Some things you just can't take back, no matter if you felt justified at the time. Wedding days should be off-limits for outbursts. If you can't act like an adult, get a babysitter.

# Alcohol doesn't make all parties more fun

I had a bride that I loved a little more than most. She came by often to touch base on wedding planning and we always ended up spending a couple of hours talking about anything and everything. She was adorable and we made each other laugh. A lot. I looked forward to her event for almost a year – it would be one of the best events of our season.

I had met the groom once or twice, so I didn't have a close

relationship with him like I did the bride. She gushed over him and their love story often, so I loved him because she did.

Her wedding day arrived. Everyone was excited that it was finally here – the bride and I were like two college roommates the way we giggled and carried on that day. It was a large wedding with a lot of moving parts, so there was a considerable amount of staff on hand that day.

The party went on without a hitch. All the vendors did what they were hired to do and everyone was having a good time. Because I had scheduled the bartender and security guard for the couple, I sought them out to collect payment for the workers. The bride indicated that the groom had their cash.

When I found the groom, he had an excessive amount of alcohol to drink. When I asked him for their payment, he decided that it would be a good time to tell me everything he didn't like about each of them. Mind you, he had been bellied up to the bar yucking it up with the bartender all night long. They seemed like long lost friends…until it came time to pay him.

Because our venue limits the amount and types of alcohol that can be served, we deal mostly with canned/bottled beers. And because we don't want to be responsible for the taps, we ask the bridal parties to tap their own kegs. The bartender made the fatal mistake in his effort to be chatty to share that he had never tapped a keg. Apparently this didn't sit well with the groom, but he didn't say anything until he was drunk and asked to pay.

He also took exception to the location of the security guard. We station him at the front gate to keep wedding guests from taking open containers off the property. The groom had been going into the back alley (off the service entrance) to smoke and had taken his beers out there. He was angry that nobody had stopped him from doing so.

Because his bride and I had endless discussions on how things worked and why things worked a certain way, I hadn't realized that she had not shared these things with him. He was angry about things that had been thoroughly explained, just not to him.

He then insisted that I was trying to make money on the payment of the bar and security staff and he didn't want me skimming their payment. (Again, something that was discussed – I never take a cut.) So he insisted on paying them himself. Which actually turned into him yelling at my staff at the top of his lungs and refusing to pay them.

I stepped in to stop the rants and told him that if he didn't pay them, I would. But the staff was getting paid. He turned on me to the point I thought he was going to hit me. The bride was now in full panic mode seeing him engaging with me, so she grabbed her dad to have him drag her new – and very drunk – husband out of the facility.

She came to me and crumbled into a mess of tears that he had done that to me. She wanted me to know that she loved me and everything for her day was perfect – except for the last ten minutes. It was absolutely heartbreaking. We both thought we would be friends for life, but his drunk antics prevented that. I still miss her and hope she's doing well.

# Baby on board

One thing that has changed a whole lot in the last several decades is the prominence of pregnant brides. Gone are the days that an unwed pregnant girl was shipped off to an undisclosed location to "take care of an ailing aunt" for several months. People are generally accepting or at least keep a little quieter than in the past. As with everything, there are exceptions.

> When lacing a bride into her gown, I can tell by the way it pulls if she's pregnant or not.

At one wedding here, it was particularly cold outside where the wedding was being held. The bride was barely pregnant and not many people knew. But grandma did. And the secret was killing her. Because it was cold, she came indoors during the ceremony and watched with me out the window. She started with a benign, "It's very cold out there for [the bride]." I agreed with her, the bride was wearing a strapless gown. Then she amped up her alarms to include "pregnant girls shouldn't chill like that" and "isn't anyone worrying about the baby?" Since I didn't actually know that the bride was pregnant, nor could I actually do anything about the cold OR stop the ceremony because of it, I just told grandma that I'm sure she would be fine.

Sometimes I can tell the bride is prgenant when the she hasn't told anyone. When lacing a bride into her gown, I can tell by the way it pulls if she's pregnant or not. Fat can be squished or moved when pulling lacing tight. Baby doesn't give. I've leaned into a bride and asked if she was pregnant, only to have her panic. "How do you know? How can you tell? Do you think my mom can tell?" I explain why I know and assure them that it's all good.

Then there are brides who own the entire idea and wear a maternity wedding gown. In the last century, that would've been enough to have the neighborhood ladies forming a coalition against the industry. Today it is its own industry.

We also have brides who will just wait until after the baby comes and include them in their ceremonies. Nothing is sweeter than having a little baby join their parents in a little wagon decorated to match the wedding.

19

The best part of all of this is one thing…babies. Let's celebrate them. Even if their timing is less that what the grandmas deem as appropriate.

# Bachelor parties the night before the wedding are a BAD idea

I'm sure you've all heard the horror stories of groomsmen putting the drunken groom on a train and he wakes up hundreds of miles and hours away from his bride. We've all heard the stories of new tattoos, indelible marker and broken noses from bar fights. Urban legends? Maybe. Although it doesn't happen often – it does happen.

One season, I had a bride show up in a beat-up car I had never seen her in before. She was moody and cranky when she got out of the car. She was quick to tell me she wasn't mad at me, but that I had no idea what she had been through. (Honestly, I thought it was the usual last-minute bride stuff where you simply run out of time and forget to go to sleep that night.)

She then proceeded to tell me of her 3:00 a.m. phone call from a local law enforcement officer. He wanted to know if she was getting married that morning. She said yes. The officer told her that he had arrested the groom for DUI (driving under the influence of alcohol) and that he had been yelling from the back seat about not going to jail, he was getting married in a few hours. He just wanted to verify the story.

When she verified the story, the officer (obviously a softie) asked if she would be willing to take responsibility for him and he would not take him to jail. However, her car (that the groom was driving) had already been towed. And he would still have a DUI on record and have to see the judge early Monday morning.

After this close call with the law, the bride was now stuck with a drunk, slobbery man afraid that she was either going to kill him or not marry him. (I actually think he was unable to decide which would be worse.) He kept her up for the rest of the night begging her to marry him and asking her if she was going to leave him at the altar.

As it turns out – he sobered up and she showed up. And a good time was had by all.

# Birth moms

There are so many scenarios that place children with adults other than their birth parents. These scenarios can range from the birth mom opting to place her baby for adoption to the state removing the baby from the mother. Whatever the case, there is usually always pain involved for all or most parties.

Eventually those adopted babies grow into brides and grooms. And a lot of these brides and grooms have searched for and found their birth parents and have various levels of relationships with them. When planning the wedding, these relationships can become a point of stress for all parties. Nobody wants to hurt the feelings of "birth mom" versus "adoptive mom". It can really be a difficult place for the bride and groom to be in.

We've had weddings where the birth mom was an invited guest. Period. She had no expectations to be anything more than included.

We've had weddings where the birth mom was an in invited guest, but wanted to be more. And made a stink about thinking she somehow deserved more. This turns into a very touchy situation for brides and grooms who are trying to defend their own wishes and their adoptive parents, while trying not to spin the birth mother out.

One particular wedding will stand out as the birth mother from hell. The bride hadn't made public that she was adopted. She wasn't ashamed of it, she just never considered anyone besides her adoptive parents as her parents. She (and her brother) had been removed from the birth mother by the state and placed with separate families. In her twenties, she had located her brother, then her birth mother, but most importantly – her other siblings. Having been raised as an only child – her siblings were very important to her.

When it came time to plan her wedding, the drama started. Why couldn't birth mom have a role? An opinion? A day at the bridal gown shop? These were things the bride reserved for her adoptive mom – the woman who raised her.

The pressure mounted with bio mom (now aptly nicknamed "bio-hazard") with regards to whether the siblings would be able to attend the wedding. So the bride and groom extended an invitation to bio mom and her husband with a warning that they were invited guests – nothing else.

When the wedding day rolled around, my staff and I had all been put on red-alert status that "bio-hazard" was pulling out all of the stops. She had done everything in her limited power to make sure that she was heard and recognized. She even made it her mission to tell folks at the wedding that her two children had been "kidnapped" by the adoptive mothers. And when the DJ was introducing the bridal party and parents – she stomped off in a huff since she hadn't been mentioned. When it came time for the toasts, all hands on deck made sure she didn't gain control of the microphone.

By the end of the night, the families, my staff and the vendors were exhausted from trying to keep this woman in check.

If you or someone you know has been adopted and has made contact with the birth parents, be very clear to all parties what the expectations are. And be VERY cautious of the feelings of the adoptive parents. Our society has a way of making them feel like they're not "real" parents. I assure you – they are more "real" that a lot of birth parents. They had to work MUCH harder to bring a baby into their lives than most of us.

# Blended families

In today's society, it's very rare to find a marrying couple who has retained their original set of married parents. These dynamics can cause a lot of stress and worry for brides and grooms planning their special day. Weddings have the tendency to bring out certain feelings anyway – people tend to be extra sensitive about being slighted in the very least. This could be anything from the bride and groom not taking their advice on something, to their role in the wedding.

The mom versus step-mom dynamic is one that tends to be one of the hardest ones. Women, by nature, are competitive with other women. I don't like it, but it tends to be true. The mother of the bride traditionally gets a prime role in the planning and day of the celebration. If nothing else, she gets to sit on the front row. Etiquette dictates that the step-mother sits in the row behind the mother. Etiquette also dictates that the biological parents sit on the front row – married or not -- and the step-parents sit behind them. I tend to bend that rule just a bit and have the bride's (or groom's) mother sit on the front row with her current husband. Moms are the number two belles at the ball here.

The dad versus step-dad dynamic is one that causes the bride the most heartburn. She has to choose which one walks her down the aisle. This is completely based on her relationship with both men. I've seen it done any number of ways – to include having them both walk her down. One way is to have

24

her father walk her to a certain point and have her stepfather
pick up halfway down the aisle. This can be representative of
her actual life with these men. I've also seen the bride in the
middle and a dad on each arm. Sometimes the father hasn't
been in the picture for so long, the stepfather fulfills the entire
role.

There are times when the bride doesn't have a father-figure
in her life or simply chooses not to engage in the debate on
who escorts her. Our fix for that is simple and people tend to
love it. We send the groom to the altar (gazebo) with the officiant and his groomsmen. After the bridesmaids have made
their way down, the bride will make her entrance through the
doors. At that time, the groom walks back up to aisle to gather
his bride, then they walk to the altar together. It ends up being
a very sweet, touching and unexpected moment. And the bride
doesn't have to go it alone.

The blending of families will also produce half-siblings,
step-siblings and extra sets of grandparents. Wedding couples
tend to feel like everyone needs to be included in everything
so as not to hurt feelings. These inclusions should always be
based on the couple's individual relationships with these people. If the bride is closer to her half-sister than her full sister,
then she should be the maid of honor. Nothing dictates who
stands where and who fills what role. They should all be based
on what feels right – not whose feelings will be hurt more.

The long and short of wedding planning is this – you are go-

ing to hurt someone's feelings. Probably more than one someone. Plan your day as you see fit without intentionally hurting
anyone's feelings. Everyone will be fine. Eventually.

# You've had four of his children – get down there and marry him!

When the name showed up on my office caller ID, I remember thinking, "That name looks like the popular football player
from my high school." We had a nice conversation, he scheduled an appointment and I remembered wondering if I would
recognize him when he got here. I did.

The funny thing is, I had in my mind that he was the ultra-
popular, stuck-up guy from my school. But when he and his
sweet bride got here – I realized that "shy" and "stuck up" look
mostly the same from the outside. And… it had been at least
20 years.

He and his bride had been together for a very long time.
They had four beautiful kids together and finally decided to
make it official. We went through the wedding planning and
had a great time getting to know each other. I told the bride
how he was the hot ticket in high school, but I had kept a safe
distance because he was popular and I wasn't. I never really
knew him – only the legend.

As the wedding day rolled around, the bride was very nervous. She was pacing and nearly hyperventilating. I always
stay back with the bride while I send everyone else down the

aisle. I tried my usual pep talks – telling her she was beautiful. Telling her how fabulous her dress was. Complimenting her on her children. She was still having a hard time making that first step out the door. I finally said to her, "You've had four of his children. Get down there and marry him! Or I will!"

That got the laugh I needed out of her and I sent her down the aisle. And I didn't even have to remind her that I was already happily married.

# Who was supposed get the bride to the venue?

Our bride was meticulous in her planning. We had several meetings on how things would go. We discussed color in depth and carried color swatches out into the sun to make sure they were still the same color. The rehearsal was carried out with military precision and the "to do" lists were distributed to each bridesmaid and groomsman after the rehearsal with stern words on how they were to be carried out. Don't get me wrong, the bride was not a bridezilla on any level. She knew what she wanted and delegated with the efficiency of upper management. She was very sweet to work with and had a handle on everything.

Fast forward to her wedding day. Bridesmaids arrive and immediately jump into the functions of getting dressed in the bride's room. The groomsmen arrive, diligently sporting the items they were enlisted to provide. The musicians, minister, photographer, etc. were all filing in at their designated times. As the coordinator, I was keeping my finger on the multiple pulses going on around the property. But the one heartbeat missing was the bride's. Without sounding any alarms, I would casually ask the bridesmaids if anyone had heard from her. No. I asked the groomsmen if everything was going okay. Yes. The bride's parents arrived. No bride. I asked if they knew where she was. No.

The buzz of the day continued moving on and getting louder with every passing minute. Once again, I started the rounds of asking if anyone had heard from her. I called her cell phone. No answer. Now I'm starting to wonder if she's coming at all. And if not, why? Did she run? Did something terrible happen? Should I sound the alarms?

The wedding start time was approaching quickly. The clock ticked louder and louder in my head, yet nobody seemed alarmed at all that the bride was nowhere to be found.

It's 6:00 p.m. Start time. Now we're at critical mass. I'm standing in the main room wondering what my next move is. Do I go to the groom and tell him his bride isn't here? Do I ask the bridesmaids one more time to call her? Do I put her mother into a panic by suggesting that something might be wrong? Then something moved out of the corner of my eye. I turned my head towards it. I bent down to get a better look out of the front window. There is was. A big yellow taxi. And a VERY mad bride.

Before I could formulate a sentence, she barreled through the door, two fists full of wedding gown and said, "Let's do this before I change my mind." I do not exaggerate when I tell you she flew out of the taxi and directly down the aisle.

I'm stunned beyond words. What the heck just happened? Had I crossed into the Twilight Zone? As it turns out, she hadn't added "get the bride to the venue" on anyone's list. Therefore, nobody did. Problem was, the list had things like "pick up car, take to hotel", "cell phones are off limits" and other similar "dos & don'ts". The car had been picked up and dropped off at the hotel. And the cell phones had been promptly turned off when they arrived at the venue – rendering the bride's calls for help completely useless. No car. No phone. No clue what to do next. Next idea? Call a taxi. Then wait. Now, who gets to be mad at whom? I don't think there's a flowchart for that one.

Lists. They can be good for keeping order and useful tools. They can also turn the best of intentions into the worst of outcomes. Use them wisely.

# In your FaceBook

One of the newest innovations as of late is social networking. Many people use it as a means to reconnect with old friends and to stay connected with current friends and families. As a business owner, I use it to connect with my brides – past, current and future. I see it as a place that future brides can find me and verify my personality. It's a place I can keep up with past brides and their lives. And I love getting to know my couples through the wedding planning process using Facebook.

I've recently witnessed what I will refer to as "terror" unfolding right before my eyes. I had been "friended" by both the bride and the groom. About four months after they had signed their contract, the groom contacted me and said he was calling off the wedding because he felt the bride was stringing him along and just not ready to commit. He was completely heartbroken and felt like he was walking away from the love of his life, but felt he had to do it.

I kept in touch with him through messages and chats because I knew he was really struggling. I also watched the bride through Facebook posts and photos move on with her life with a new boyfriend (almost immediately), a new house and a lot of "I love life" stuff. I had also noticed (through snooping, of course) that they had un-friended each other – which I was glad to see because I didn't want this sweet guy to have to see her posts and pictures.

Their wedding date came and went. I didn't bring any attention to it because I didn't know what state of mind he was in.

Then about 10 days after their contracted wedding date – I see a "status change" on Facebook that the guy had changed his status to "married" to another girl. But prior to the status change, he had re-friended the ex-fiancé and friended the new wife (which incidentally showed up as a single status change). Then promptly changed his status to married to the new girl.

(Side note: the ex-bride had status changed from "in a relationship" to "single" to "in a relationship" – the last relationship did not list the guy, but a wall post from a friend mentioned the name of her ex-fiancé and plans for a getaway weekend. I couldn't help but wonder if she thought they were getting back together...)

To clear up any confusion, he followed with a posting that he felt right about her and married her quickly and not many people knew or could've stopped him. There were many comments below the posting wishing him the best and congratulating him.

Knowing two of the players in this game, I would not be quick to say any of these moves were intentional. They are wonderful people with wonderful families and hearts of gold. But I believe they caused damage nonetheless.

Remember: social media sites can be good. They can also cause heartbreak. And in a few easy clicks, even someone like I am can follow the activity. Sometimes it just doesn't look good.

# If you've been married four times – you know what awaits you at the end of the aisle

It happens. Sometimes we don't get it right the first time. Others end up married multiple times before they figure it out.

I had a very wonderful couple. They were both in their early fifties and had been married multiple times each. I try very hard to not judge the path that folks have taken to get to me – we never know the paths or the pain that brought them here. And it's a VERY different dynamic than twenty-somethings getting married right out of college.

The bride had given herself an ulcer. Literally. To the point that she ended up needing to special order a meal for herself from the caterer because the red sauce she ordered for her guests would not have worked for her. She had worried herself into a real physical tizzy.

On the day of the wedding, she seemed to be doing okay. She was the usual nervous, if not just a little more than most. She paced and rocked and wanted a cigarette. And another. And another. The groom seemed fine.

When it came time to start the ceremony, we got everyone lined up and ready to go. The procession went on as rehearsed. When it came time for the bride to go down the aisle – she stopped. She just stood there. The music kept playing. I looked over at one of my employees with the what-am-I-supposed-to-do look. The bride took a deep breath, looked at the front door, then rocked back on her heels. I knew for a fact she was going to run. But she didn't. She rocked back to get enough momentum to thrust herself out the door and get herself down the aisle. The amount of relief that washed over me was intense. I had never had a runaway bride.

As she and the groom came back down the aisle and headed in to sign their marriage license, she said, "I don't know what that was all about. It's not like I don't know what awaited at the end of that aisle."

In today's world where marriages are less likely to be arranged, we have to remember that WE choose our mate and WE choose to say "yes". We'll also choose to walk down that aisle to meet them. What comes after that is up to both of us. Getting down the aisle is the easy part. Don't make it too hard.

*Getting down the aisle is the easy part*

# Mixed cultures

Oh, where to start?

This one can get really touchy really fast. Generally speaking, our mothers want us to marry someone from our same town/religion/culture/race. It's how they have played it out in their minds since we were born. When we introduce something different, it is often met with some resistance.

Religion is an easy one to start with. Our families are a lot of times well rooted in our religions. Generations of families identify as a particular religion and it's very hard for them to see it any other way. It can get particularly troublesome for families when the religions are opposite in nature – they tend to put up bigger fights thinking they will lose you to "the other side". Over the years, I have seen a great shift in people being either non-religious or of no particular religion. It's a shift that is very hard for families to grasp. And in a world where love is harder and harder to find, people are a little less willing to let it be a deal-breaker.

Mixing races or cultures is a hard one. Again, our families wish for us to meet a nice guy/girl that was raised like we were. When a different culture is introduced into our worlds, it's sometimes very hard to swallow – mostly because of the unknown. They celebrate different things for different reasons. And once we get to know them, they're not quite as scary anymore.

It's very hard for Greek/Hispanic/African American families to "let" one of their own marry outside of their culture. They sometimes manifest their dislike in a variety of ways. I see it happen when the groom is of these descents. The mother of the groom will engage in a bizarre ritual of making him choose. It can be as subtle as her being incredibly late for the wedding and seeing if he'll wait for her to begin the ceremony. If he'll ask his bride to wait just a little longer. Or if he will side with his bride and start without his mother (and siblings). It's a heartbreaking thing to watch and a glimpse into what dynamic these families will engage in.

Because we do not limit our engagements with people, we get to see myriad beautiful love stories unfold here. We've seen same sex couples show love to each other and their families in a world where they are still not universally accepted. We've seen Jews marry Catholics and whites marry blacks and Native Americans marry gingers. To us it's all love and it should all be celebrated.

# My invitation ink doesn't match my bridesmaid dresses

It really happened. Early in my career of wedding planning and owning my venue, I had a bride call me in tears begging me to let her come by the office. (Of course, I thought the worse – break-up, bounced check, lost job, car accident, etc.) I told her to get right in and we'll figure out what needed to be done based on the crisis at hand. When she got here, she shoved a beautifully embossed wedding invitation into my hand and blurted, "LOOK!"

I read it. Then read it again – expecting to see a misspelling, or an ex's name or something, but I couldn't find anything wrong with it. It was printed straight. The spacing seemed to be fine. I must have had a dumb look on my face because she then spouted, "The ink doesn't match my bridesmaid's dresses!"

Since I was holding the invitation, but not the bridesmaid's dress – I couldn't dispute this point with her. But clearly she was upset about this. The ink was black. It wasn't orange or turquoise or something blatantly obvious – just plain ol' black.

So, in my effort to calm her down I told her how beautiful the invitation was, how well-worded it was, etc., etc. She continued to cry and point at it. At my wits end I said, "Do you know what this means?!"

She sniffed and looked up. (I'm sure she was expecting something brilliant.)

I said, "It means a DISCOUNT!"

She said, "What do you mean?"

I explained to her that because they had not been printed the way they had been ordered, the vendor owed her a discount or a reprint. She opted for the discount. Apparently, the color wasn't as important as she had originally thought.

# If you regret marrying your wife – don't tell the bartender at your wedding

I know. It seems like a pretty obvious piece of advice. But obviously it needs to be addressed.

The couple was a regular couple. They had been together for several years. They planned their wedding with friends and family. It didn't feel like a contentious event – the same amount of planning, budgeting and color conversations happened as usual.

If I remember correctly, the bride and groom were in their late twenties, possibly early thirties. They had both been in previous marriages/relationships. I believe they may have even had a couple of kids they brought into the marriage.

The day went on as planned. Wedding party here on time. Ceremony started when it should have. Dinner served. Dancing. Cake cutting. Bouquet tossing. It all seemed to be going as planned.

Somewhere in the midst of these festivities, the bartender called me over. She began to tell me of the attention she was getting from the groom. He had been drinking. A lot. And as he continued to visit her repeatedly for his refills, he started to tell her of his woes. The kids. The job. The wedding. Then he said it – he wished he hadn't married her.

Thankfully, I have no real recollection of who it was or really even when it was. I just hope that it was the drunk's version of cold feet, not real regret.

But just for the record, don't tell the bartender. Or even the DJ. If you made a bad choice – work it out later. We're just here to make your day the best we can.

# I wasn't raised in your culture/religion/household – please explain it to me

All of us were raised in homes that we considered "normal". They were normal to us. Our parents are educated or not. They can be die-hard alumni of a prestigious college. Or graduates from the School of Hard Knocks. We come from a variety of religious and cultural backgrounds.

The rituals of marriage vary by family, culture, religion and preference. Our cultures also vary by parts of the world or parts of the country that we hail from.

When it comes to wedding planning, you must be specific about what your beliefs, traditions, superstitions, religious preferences, etc. are.

**Religion:** Many religions have very specific "rules" – whether they are regarding lifestyles (abstinence from pre-marital relations or alcohol), to the order of ceremonies and prayers. Just because we don't know what they are doesn't mean that we have an opinion about them. We just need to know so as not to be offensive. An example that comes to mind was a Jehovah's Witness family. They were very sweet and very forthcoming with their preferences. My confusion came with the champagne and the toast. They brought champagne and glasses and the best man had prepared a toast, but it wasn't something that they did simultaneously. It took me a few minutes to get that out of the bride, but once I did – we were able to get down to business.

Mormon families abstain from alcohol and don't have any at their events. There are also norms associated with appropriate dress and music.

**Culture:** Many cultures have traditions during the ceremony. From coins, lassos and broom jumping – we've seen it all. But keep in mind – we had to see it once before we knew what it was. And someone always has to be first.

**Superstitions:** There are so many! Seeing the bride before the wedding. Coin in the shoe. Something old, new, borrowed, blue. And any number of personal superstitions that are brought to the party. Speak up – we don't know what bad things happen if you step on a crack.

**Same sex:** These weddings are typically not considered "traditional", but many of our same sex couples try to keep their weddings as traditional as possible. Most of our questions with regards to same sex weddings came in the form of logistics – who gets to use the bride's room? Two dresses?

Two tuxes?  A mixture of both?  We just need to know how to best accommodate you.

# Ring-side seats

Because I've owned a wedding venue for twenty years, I've gotten a ringside seat to the greatest celebrations of love.  Here are a few that stood out for the best reasons.

Kenya – We had a lovely couple that had recently immigrated from Kenya and wanted to be married.  They chose very "American" traditions, from their clothing to their vows and everything in between.  As the officiant pronounced them husband and wife, the family members in the audience started in with the most beautiful and celebratory singing and dancing we had ever heard.  It was pure love and joy being manifested in the most amazing way.  The officiant and I stood back and watched it unfold in front of us.  To this day it still brings a smile to my face, tears to my eyes and a chill up my spine.

Native American – It is a widely accepted practice that Native shamans don't normally leave the reservations to perform their ceremonies.  This particular bride had gotten permission from the tribe to have him travel to her wedding.  She was marrying an African American man who was a very straight-laced stockbroker. His groomsmen were all cut from the same cloth.  During the ceremony, the shaman started his ritual.  Having grown up near a reservation, I knew a little bit about their rituals – to include what exactly goes into the "peace pipe". I was keeping my eyes on the groom as the shaman lit the pipe. As the groom got a whiff of smoke, he immediately realized what he was burning and darted his gaze to me immediately. I could tell he was trying very hard not to laugh. I mouthed to him and motioned the best I could that he could NOT laugh. I kept his gaze and we both tried to breathe normally. He managed to get through the entire ceremony without laughing, but once he got back inside with me – the peals of laughter were almost too much to handle. His bride had no idea that he had no idea. She got a good laugh out of it, too.

Disney – If not done right, this could've been tragic. But thankfully they had hired an amazing officiant whose day job is as a writer. Their entire wedding ceremony was quotes from various Disney movies. It started with the bride and groom being referred to as princess and prince with excerpts from Snow White's "Some Day My Prince Will Come". Their vows contained adapted lyrics of Little Mermaid's "I Will Always Be With You". To be rounded out with a ring exchange to Aladdin's "Whole New World". The ceremony ended with The Lion King's "Love Will Find a Way". It was one of the most amazing and romantic ceremonies ever.

Honorable Mentions:

- The bride and groom that met playing an online game. The beginning of the ceremony started with a big screen television playing the game's opening graphics. They were also dressed in costumes similar to their game characters.

41

- The biker bride who wore white denim pants, a white lace halter, clear acrylic shoes and walked down the aisle to "Highway to Hell" by AC/DC. Her bridal party were all wearing leathers and their denim club vests.

- The Halloween wedding where the bride was wearing an iridescent purple gown. Both the bride's and groom's mothers were dressed in witch costumes. The bridal party came down the aisle to The Nightmare Before Christmas.

- The Star Trek wedding where everyone came dressed as their favorite character.

# 'Thank you for accepting us'

"Thank you for accepting us." That's how she signed her email. She and her girlfriend had just booked a wedding with me. It broke my heart. These two beautiful women sat in front of me and told me their love story. It was sweet and they both shared their parts in the story like a well-written, well-rehearsed, script to a great movie. Only it wasn't. It is their life. It is their love. And it's real.

They shared with me that they were nervous about looking at wedding venues because they are a same sex couple. That sometimes they are met with ugliness and resistance. And that she had seen other same sex photos in my galleries and felt comfortable calling.

It caused me to pause and wonder why people are afraid of

those unlike them. I don't drink or smoke, but wouldn't turn away a customer who did. I also don't have tattoos or facial piercings – but some of the most amazing people I've met do. My parents aren't divorced. Should I turn away a bride whose parents are? Where does that line get drawn?

Our way of life is simple – serve those who have come to us and asked to be served. Love those who have come to us in love. What else?

Bring us your love story. We don't care if you're model perfect. Or if you're marrying a man or woman. Or if your gown isn't what we would've picked. It's YOUR happily ever after, not ours. We're just here to be a brick in the path of your journey. And we're honored to be so.

# Unaccepting families

This is a tough one. This world can be brutal. And we search the corners of it for the one that we love and that love us and we want to spend our lives with them. They understand our quirks and love us because of them, or despite them.

Most of the time, I have a front row seat to celebrations of love and family. There's always a little stress involved and some personalities are harder than others to mesh with. There are sometimes when members of some families can be so brutal I wonder if I'm being punked.

In one particular instance, the groom and his mother were at odds about his selection of his bride. She was hellbent on convincing him that he was making a grave error. He was steadfast in his commitment to marry his fiancée. I had been put on notice to keep an eye on his mother. All night I kept inventory on where the groom was, as well as his mother. At one point I lost them both and went on a quest to find them. She had dragged him into the alley and was laying into him about how he had "F-ed" his life up that night. I quickly removed him from the one-sided conversation with a made-up need for him from the photographer. I can only imagine that she made him choose that night. He chose his bride.

On another occasion, our sweet bride was pregnant and marrying a man from a different culture than hers. Just before the bride got to the venue, her parents called her and told her they wouldn't be coming. They weren't going to sit on the front row pretending to be okay with their trashy pregnant daughter marrying THAT guy. Of course, she was devastated. She sucked it up, got dressed and left her parents in her rear-view mirror.

Here's the long and short of this – if a parent or family member takes a stand like this, it can't be taken back. They could have very well sat in the front row and said nothing while brewing hatred in their own hearts. But a no-show is a no-show forever. And giving your opinion after the marriage license is signed is useless.

# Uninvited guests / restraining orders

Most people – or their families – come with a little extra baggage. Some even come with a lot. With today's family make-up, we end up with a lot of exes, steps, halves, etc. Sometimes it's really hard to determine who fills the traditional roles.

**Exes:** Lots of brides and grooms have them. They oftentimes also have kids with them. Depending on the nature of the separation, some new relationships/marriages are kept quiet until the day of. Some people are even reluctant to tell their children for fear of it being repeated. And for fear of the ex showing up and causing problems.

*All of us have at least one of those family members that we are afraid will show up.*

45

Estranged family members: Let's face it. All of us have at least one of those family members that we are afraid will show up. They're druggies or drunks or just have major personality disorders. We are afraid they are going to do that one thing that makes them infamous in our family. And there will be a camera.

**Restraining orders:** It hasn't happened often, but it has happened. Some relationships end with so much volatility that a restraining order is necessary. As a point of clarification when doing final planning with my brides, we cover the topic. And I ask for a copy. Should that person show up, we can deal with it swiftly and efficiently without bothering the guests. So far so good, we've never had to do it. But we're ready if we do.

**Step-parents:** This is sometimes the most interesting dynamic. If the biological parents are divorced and remarried, there is often underlying hurt feelings and unresolved issues. The seating chart becomes a tripping point. As does the who's-going-to-walk-me-down-the-aisle question. I spend a lot of time talking my brides though these things.

**Biological parents:**   Just because you have them doesn't mean you have a perfect core family. There are many things that drive wedges between brides, grooms and their parents. We see a lot of interracial marriages, unplanned pregnancies turned weddings, and same sex marriages that are not blessed by their families. If some family members are not a huge part of your life, they are not required to be a huge part of your wedding day. Just because there are traditions, it doesn't mean you are bound by them.

# Wedding receptions and going-away parties don't mix

She loved him. It was obvious that she did. And he loved her. It was awe-inspiring to see. It made those around them believe in love all over again. They had worked together at an engineering firm for years. They knew each other very well and had a great life planned with each other. However, there was one slight problem. He had accepted another job with an oil company and was being relocated to Oklahoma. This put the wedding plans into high gear after she agreed to move with him.

Their wedding planning had a few hiccoughs in it. Their original venue had double booked their date and sent them packing with only a few months to plan another event. I got a panicked call from a bride on the edge, but we got them squeezed in and everything was back on track. Not only were they planning a wedding, they were planning a major move and major change in their lives – all at the same time. Normally one of these would put the bravest of women hiding under the bed, coming out only to pee and restock the chocolate supply. She was doing a good job keeping everything together, yet moving forward at the same time.

The wedding was beautiful. The bride blushing. The groom doting. The food was delicious. The cake was an attraction. The DJ was keeping the mood festive. Everyone was having a great time – especially the bride and groom.

Then the first guest left.

It happens. The babysitter is getting paid by the hour. Someone has to get up early in the morning, so they cut the evening short. There's any number of reasons that people will leave a wedding reception early. But it happened. And it was a shock.

It wasn't a shock to me or the guests leaving, but to the bride, it marked the beginning of the end. She clung to them like they were life vests on a treacherous sea. Then the tears. And more tears. And yet more tears.

The party went on, yet the party was over. At least for the bride. She stood by the gate as each guest tried to leave and hung on them with the fervor of the first victim. I was heart-broken for her. It was horribly sad to watch.

Not knowing what to do, I went to tell the groom what was happening. Apparently, it was too much for him, too, but didn't want to be taken away from HIS friends.

So, this lovely, sweet couple that had the wedding day of their dreams – then suffered major heartbreak that night as they said good-bye to everyone. I'm sure it seemed like a good idea at the time, but as it turned out – it wasn't such a good idea after all.

# Who wears what?

Ah yes, the age old question of what to wear. In the era of traditions now being non-traditional, a few things still hold strong, while others are a bit more flexible:

- Only the bride wears white. Period. Anyone else wearing white is viewed in direct competition with the bride. Nobody cares if it's your favorite dress. If it's white, don't wear it.

- The bride doesn't have to wear white or any shade of white. Some of our most beautiful brides sported red, black or even purple dresses. This is your day. Shine however you want.

*The bride doesn't have to wear white or any shade of white.*

- Bridesmaids dresses/outfits are a little less scripted than usual. Gone are the days when bridesmaids were required to be carbon copies of each other. Brides are much more flexible in making sure each girl feels good about herself as to what she's wearing.

- Mothers of the bride/groom typically wear evening gowns or semi-formal dresses in a shade lighter than the bridesmaids or in a complimentary color.

- Grooms can wear anything from a full tuxedo to linen pants and a linen shirt. It all depends on the formality of the wedding. We've seen some fun variations of this with red plaid and suspenders around Christmas.

- Groomsmen are extensions of the groom and will dress very similar to him.

- Fathers of the bride/groom typically wear tuxedos or suits depending on the formality of the wedding. In less formal events, we've seen dads sport cowboy boots, jeans and hats. Whatever works for everyone works best for us!

- Flower girls can wear anything from mini versions of the bride's dress to Disney princess costumes. We've seen it all and it all works.

The best part about weddings and receptions of the new millennium is that anything goes. Couples are using this as a time to share their favorite things and show their personalities.

# Who's watching the kids?

I love kids. I have two of my own. They aren't perfect. They sometimes got out of hand around large crowds. And they loved music and dancing when they were little. They're probably just like most kids. Except that I watched them like a hawk and didn't let them out of my sight – even for one minute. I KNEW what they were capable of!

There seems to be a disconnect when it comes to parents bringing children to a formal event – like a wedding or a reception. Just because you're in a confined space with friends and family doesn't mean that your kids don't need to be watched. Or parented.

When I first realized this, it was very early in my career of owning an event venue. I had a large amount of rose bushes (28, I think) in the front of my venue. Three little girls thought it looked like a whole lot of fun to behead every single rose off those bushes to play "flower girl". When I saw it in the daylight – it was total carnage. What was even more alarming to me, was that these children had been allowed outside of the block wall (where the reception was being held) and very close to a busy street. My mom heart panics when I think of how many things could have gone wrong. So, my contract was amended to reflect that no children were allowed to be outside of the block wall.

I have also discovered that hide-and-seek is a very fun game during wedding receptions. Buffet tables and areas marked "private – no entry" are favorite places to hide. Once again, I visualize a full table of hot food and chafing dishes falling on boys who dive under the buffet table to keep from being spotted. All it would take is him catching the table leg in the dive or pulling the floor-length table cloth under with him. These children are walked back to their parents and a warning given.

Food, cake and dessert tables are very tempting to kids of all ages. Most kids think that if their mothers aren't watching, they can help themselves. Sometimes this is in the form of picking the olives out of the salad (that isn't being served yet) or sampling the frosting off of the FRONT of the wedding cake. Or just generally digging into the candy buffet or the dessert spread.

My venue happens to be housed in an old home built in 1913. So because of its age, it acts as a museum of sorts. We have a lot of antiques and old things as decorations. They are not balls to be thrown or toys to be chewed on. And my windows are original wavy glass. Yes, your kid is adorable. But all I can see is his slobbery fingers banging on my 100+ year old original glass.

We also have an antique piano in our main building. It's mostly for decoration. It can be played, except that it doesn't hold a tune very well. It baffles me at the number of mothers and grandmothers that use it as a babysitting tool. Many children and babies have been perched on the stool and allowed to bang on it indefinitely.

Children are very much a part of our families. And important parts of wedding traditions. If children and their antics are not what you envision at your reception – find an alternative. Perhaps an off-site house or hotel room where you pay a babysitter, order pizza and have crafts. Then let your guests know that free babysitting is available and that you wish for your reception to be adults only. Many people will find it offensive that their children are not invited so be prepared for that.

If children ARE included in your guest list, be sure to be clear to their parents about your expectations on behavior, containment and supervision.

# Vendors

## Who ordered the drinks?

It was my first event. November 7, 1998. I was a venue owner! I owned my own business! We had worked so hard to renovate our 1913 historic home and it was finally ready to host its first event. I had arrived at my destination goal and I was a happy girl

I knew very few things about events that day except that I loved doing them and I was going to quit my job soon and do this full time.

My bride was happy. The bride's mother was happy. We got everyone dressed. Everything was set up and decorated. We were ready to go. The photographer was snapping away with the camera and the groom was chewing off his fingernails.

We got through the ceremony with the precision of a well-oiled machine. The reset between the wedding and reception went off without a hitch. The bride and groom were smiling radiantly while the photographer finished snapping photos to commemorate this fabulous occasion (hers and mine).

We flowed flawlessly from the photographs into dinner. The DJ was right on cue with the introductions of the bridal party and the new Mr. and Mrs. This was so much fun!! (Did I mention that I'm a venue owner? And I now own my own business?) I was the queen of my world!

The bride had chosen a Mexican buffet as her dinner offering. Since we allow outside catering, they had taken care of it themselves. It smelled wonderful and the guests were digging in with great gusto.

I was standing there trying to look important, yet helpful when the first guest said, "Where can I find the drinks?"

"Ummmm… let me check for you," I said as I looked around wondering to myself where they were. Not finding any myself, I went to the caterer to ask. With my inability to speak Spanish and her limited ability to speak English – we determined that drinks had not been ordered. What? How does that happen? Didn't you offer them? Yes, the bride said her mother told her to order food, but didn't say anything about drinks.

As fun as the placing-the-blame game is to play, it still doesn't change the fact that there are no drinks to be found anywhere. And then the line started forming: "Can I get some water?"; "This food is really spicy, I need something to drink NOW!"; "What do you mean there are no drinks?"

It was like a bad dream with hordes of angry people with their mouths on fire coming at me with the gusto of the passengers on the Titanic looking for an available life raft. I'M NOT TRAINED! WHAT AM I SUPPOSED TO DO?

So, this is where the rubber hits the road. Grab a pitcher, grab a container of Countrytime lemonade, chip the ice from the bottom of the tray – let's make something happen. Send my husband to the oriental market to get something wet – anything. Just go.

The lemonade mix, the red gooey junk he found at the market, water and ice all went into a big bowl served in leftover birthday cups. Tragedy averted. Fires extinguished. All is calm on the western front.

Now we ask who is ordering the drinks? Are you sure? And just to make darned sure, I always follow up with the caterer prior to the event. "No surprises" is an easier thing to manage than "adapt and overcome". We can do both, but we're much more efficient about it now.

# Meet with your officiant – make sure he / she knows your last name

It happens. Brides and grooms plan the "wedding" – usually a general term used to describe the day, not the actual ceremony. A lot of times, the ceremony gets overlooked as a non-essential detail. This usually means that the officiant/minister/judge is trying to come up with your ceremony without any input from you. If this is the case, your rights to be disappointed have been waived.

I had an Asian couple with unusual (for Americans) first names and single syllable last names. Their officiant had never met them and was flying blind with their expectations. (I will also add that he didn't appear to be diligent in his own findings to make sure he got it right.)

Halfway through the ceremony, he confused himself as to which name belonged to which person. He stared blindly at his book for what seemed like a long time – honestly, it was probably only 30 seconds that passed, but as dead air, it felt longer. When he finally recovered from that, we all breathed a sigh of relief.

At the end of the ceremony, he invited the groom to kiss the bride and introduced them as Mr. and Mrs. McKenzie… Uh, what happened to the single syllable Asian last name? The bride whispered to him (loud enough for the microphone to capture it), "That's not our name!"

Once again, we got a blank stare and dead air. The bride and groom finally gave up, we started the recessional music and they proceeded back down the aisle.

As we got back inside to sign the marriage license, the officiant did what any red-blooded American man would do. He blamed it on his wife.

# Without a license – it's just another prom night

It happens. As brides, we tend to get caught up in the details of our "wedding", which actually isn't the wedding at all. It's the accumulation of everything for our wedding DAY.

We have dates and bridesmaids to choose. When we get dates and people, we need dresses and tuxes. And not just bride and groom dresses and tuxes – bridesmaids, groomsmen, flower girls, ring bearers, parents, siblings, etc. Everything has to be perfect!

Then we get into vendors – officiant, caterer, baker, photographer, videographer, DJ – the list goes on and on. We need menus and cake flavors and playlists and photo lists and engagement photos. But let's not forget invitations and party favors and, and, and… it just never ends.

Most brides and grooms have jobs. Or school. Or both. We have budgets and time constraints. Sometimes we have state lines that need to be crossed. We also have countless well-wishing folks giving us their opinions. Do this. Don't do that. I should've done this. I shouldn't have done that. I'm not paying for this. I'm paying for that.

As brides, we try so hard to not offend anyone. Bridesmaids, sisters, mothers, future mothers-in-law. And it seems like everyone wants a piece of the bride – her time, her attention, her money, her commitment. So is it any wonder that sometimes things fall through the cracks?

It has happened here several times. Part of my regular rotation is touching base with the bride when she arrives on site. I hang her dress up. Ask her any final questions I may have. Answer any questions she may have. Collect the accessory items (guest book, party favors, etc.) to get them placed where they belong. I also always ask for the marriage license. Most times, they provide it immediately, or tell me who it has been assigned to. Sometimes I get a blank stare. I recognize it almost immediately. They forgot about the license. THEY. FORGOT. ABOUT. THE. LICENSE.

At this stage in the game, we have no options. It's the weekend, the courts are closed, it's after 5:00 p.m., the wedding starts in 10 minutes – and a thousand other reasons. There's quite literally nothing that can be done right now. Except get married anyway. You can still walk down the aisle and repeat your vows to each other. You can still eat dinner, cut cake and toast champagne. You can even dance your first dances as husband and wife. But you can't be legally married that day.

The laws in the state of Arizona require that the license be present at the time of the ceremony, as well as the witnesses and the proclamation (the "I do"). Licenses cannot be post- or pre-dated to accommodate this snafu. Once the license has been obtained, the officiant, bride, groom and two witnesses must gather again to make it legal – on your legal wedding date.

To some this is devastating – the date was significant for any number of reasons. Now this. How did this happen? It's a tough start to your married life – mostly because you'll be tough on yourself for forgetting such an important piece.

So in Arizona, your license is good for one year from the date of issue. Put it where you can see it. Even if you forget it at home – we can send someone for it.

If not, we'll have a fun night – just like prom night. And the bride and groom will be treated like royalty. Then you'll have to make it legal some other day. Whether you tell your family or not is entirely up to you.

*So in Arizona, your license is good for one year from the date of issue. Go get it.*

# Venues closing

It's happened yet again. A wedding venue has closed right as the spring season is upon us. I'm not sure why it affects me the way it does – less competition for me, right? Sure, but there's more...there are some very sweet brides and doting grooms that just had their worlds rocked. And that's not okay.

Because I'm the curious type, I searched the name of the venue that closed. It's beautiful. Absolutely. I've admired it since it opened about two years ago. But looking at the reviews online, I'm wondering why people who clearly don't like people get in the people business? It seems counter-intuitive to me. If I even had one bad review online, I wouldn't be able to sleep until I got it right, then made it right for that reviewer.

The rule of starting your own business is "find something you love to do and you'll never have to work a day in your life." The addendum to that is... do something you would do, even if you weren't getting paid to do it. That's a reality. A cold hard fact. There were many years in the beginning that we put more money in that we got out. But it was my dream and I loved it. And that trumped the make-a-million-dollars-by-the-time-I'm-35-years-old-thing. Every. Single. Day. And more than two decades later – I'm still doing what I love.

I've been in business since 1998. My paperwork says 1997, that's when everything was filed, but the first bride I sent down the aisle was November 7, 1998. We made some mistakes.

We had some kinks. But we also did everything in our power to make that bride feel as special as we could. And that's something we've done every day since.

I had "wedding professionals" early on tell me that I would "fail quickly" because I refused to be like everyone else. I didn't want to charge too much, charge extra for every little thing, nickel and dime people to death, then tack on fees, taxes and gratuities. To those who doubted me... I'm still here. And I still don't charge extra fees. I even eat the tax. The book-keeping and awkward conversations are not worth it to me. I'm flexible, I'm personal and I care. Really. Once again... I'm still here.

I'm not saying we're perfect – we're definitely not. But I've met some of the most amazing couples and their families that have enriched my life more than I could ever put into words. Thanks to social media, I've been able to watch my couples buy new homes, welcome new babies, graduate from college, welcome more babies and remain a part of their lives. I've gotten a couple of very sad cards and calls from those who have lost their loved ones – and I'm flattered beyond belief that they thought to call/write so I would know of the loss. After all, I'm just the wedding venue coordinator, right?

My venue turned 100 years old a handful of years ago. It's not the most perfect venue; it's got 100 years of wear, tear and Arizona summers under its belt. But it's full of love. And I mean full. We named the business after Virginia Hook – the sweet elderly lady that we purchased her home from. We kept in touch with her until her death just a few years ago. In our early years, she wanted me to call before every wedding so she could talk to our brides – she told them loved lived here and they could take some with them. Her family has been here and held events here. They said, "I knew you would be here" when I showed up at her funeral.

We've touched every single corner of this historic house, we've lovingly restored every single corner of it, and because it's 100 years old – that process never ends. It's also my home. We live above "the shop" and we've raised our family here. We're not going anywhere. It's not just a job, it's our life. And we have saved this gem of a home from the wrecking ball. It's going to take a pretty big army of men to drag me away from here. I've invested blood, sweat, tears and my family. Who could walk away from that? Not me.

So… if you know someone who had their venue pull the rug out from under them – send them my way. I won't add insult to injury. And I'll love them like my own.

# A sand ceremony sounds lovely – what do you mean 'where's the sand'?

Brides and grooms have been including unity ceremonies within their wedding ceremonies forever. The traditional contemporary unity ceremony is a unity candle – a large pillar candle with two taper candles on each side. The large candle represents the marriage – the two side candles each represent the bride and groom. When the center candle is lit with the two outer candles – it is meant to signify the unification of the couple. (A fun fact is that the "unity candle" was first introduced in a soap opera wedding, and has since become a part of our culture.)

There are many other ceremonies that have been adapted from this general premise. One of the newer versions ("newer" meaning in this century) of a unity ceremony is the sand ceremony. It can be done with two colors of sand – one for each person being married. We also use it for blended families where everybody has their own color of sand. The individual vials of sand represent each member of the family. During the sand ceremony, each person pours their vial of sand into a larger vessel – representing the coming together of the families. The explanation typically has something to do with the visual blending of the colors, but everyone keeping their individual personalities. And that if the vessel was to be dumped out – it would be nearly impossible to separate the colors of sand from each other.

One particular wedding that I can recall, I went to the bride to collect her ceremony things – marriage license, memorial items, etc. I had noted that they would be doing a sand ceremony, so I asked her about her sand. The look on her face told me everything I needed to know. She hadn't thought to bring the sand.

Adapt and overcome. It's what we do. I collected up the officiant and told her of our "situation". We hit the kitchen and began to dig through cabinets. We had considered sugar and coffee – just so there would be a color distinction, but the ground coffee poured at a different rate than did the sugar. As we stood there laughing about it – we decided that they were both very sweet and sugar would suffice for them both.

And it did.

# I tried to book my own vow renewal

Yep. Operative word – TRIED. Not one here at Virginia's House. I wanted to be a customer and book a vow renewal on Maui as a surprise to my husband for our 20th Anniversary. I booked the trip, made a lot of decisions, spent a lot of money and relied heavily on my travel agent. (She's fabulous, by the way.)

My travel agent researched my vow renewal options and spoke to the officiant directly. She gave him my number, me his number, etc. He did try to call me twice, but both times my husband was with me (remember, I wanted this to be a surprise), so I didn't answer. So, I went to the Maui wedding website and tried to communicate with the officiant using email. The website was relatively easy to get around, but I was confused about beach permits, etc. I emailed the officiant asking for clarification on beach permits and the dates he had available. He responded that everything was spelled out specifically on his website AND he required that I be at a desktop, on his website and on the phone with him simultaneously to identify available dates. I responded that I just needed clarification because his website was a bit confusing to me – he responded AGAIN that his website was crystal clear and that he wouldn't provide me with available dates until I was on a computer on his website and on the phone with him. Did I mention we were heading into a holiday weekend? And that I was not going to be near the three required pieces of equipment simultaneously for nearly a week? I think I emailed the same basic short list (permits and dates) up to four times. And got the same response. Every. Single. Time.

Needless to say, the idea of a vow renewal no longer has the romance I had envisioned attached to it. I scrapped the idea out of sheer frustration. I guess I assumed that people do business the way Jody Serey (Spirit and Light) and I do. Clearly not.

At Virginia's House, we will communicate with you on your preferred medium. I have Skyped with a soldier in Iraq and showed him around the venue. I have texted college students across the country. I have spoken on the phone with distraught brides at 10pm. I have emailed never-ending answers to brides with never-ending questions just to make them comfortable. Jody of Spirit and Light operates the same way. We will meet you where you are and how you are to make you comfortable with the process. And we don't like stress or allow panic. This is the best way we know how to combat both.

So, to the vow renewing officiant on Maui – best of luck to you. Your website isn't as clear as you'd think. And I won't be meeting you on my vacation with my husband. Instead, I think I'll have Jody from Spirit and Light write me up something special, then I'll drag hubs out onto the beach and we'll say nice things to each other while the sun is setting. In fact, that sounds absolutely perfect to me.

# Wedding gowns held for ransom – and other bridal boutique horror stories

Because I'm the venue owner, I don't typically get involved in much dress hype. Don't get me wrong, we talk about gowns. I want to see pictures. And I tell them which stores I've heard good things about. And which stores I haven't. We're girls. Dresses – GOWNS – are our thing.

There are any number of things that can go wrong at a bridal boutique. I'm not bashing these owners or employees – truly, I'm not. I think that most of the time, the brides probably caused all or most of their own problems by not fully understanding what the stores' policies were or how much things cost.

**Alterations – ask questions.**

- If I buy my gown here, do I have to have it altered here? There are many different ways stores handle this. A lot of times, they make you think you have to (free money, just labor to them), but in actuality – you can buy the gown of the rack and walk out the door with it.

- If you pin it for alterations and I change my mind – is there a fee? I had a bride that went in for her alterations. The seamstress had pinned the gown, then gave her a price for alterations. The alteration price was double the price of the gown. Because of that fact, she decided that she would take her gown elsewhere. That's when the fight started. Once she took the gown off, the seamstress took the gown hostage. As it turns out, since she had spent the time pinning the gown, but wasn't going to get the alteration fee – she was charging a "pin fee". The bride called me panicked and crying. She had already paid for the gown and had the receipt, but felt like she had been thrown out of the store without the gown. She didn't know what else to do. I suggested that she go back inside and ask to speak to the owner/manager to see if a resolution could be reached. If not, she should call the police. Honestly, I don't remember how it resolved – except that she got her gown back and I learned about "pin fees".

- If I leave the store with it, can I bring it back for alterations? This is one I recently discovered. The bride left the store with the gown to seek other alteration options. When she tried to come back with it, they wouldn't even pin her because they couldn't verify where the gown came from or if anyone else had touched it.

## Custom gowns – more questions.

- Can I see photos of other gowns you have made?

- Can I talk to other brides you have made gowns for?

- What happens if you can't make the gown look right?

This didn't happen to one of my brides, but to the sister of a close friend. She had a specific style in mind. The seamstress had never sewn a wedding gown before. The bride was very thin and tall. She had gone to the home of the seamstress on several occasions for pinning, fitting, etc. When she went in for the final fitting one week prior to the wedding, she tried the dress on again. She said it was horrible – it made her look short and pregnant. The seamstress pinned and pinched and said she knew what was going on and could fix it. When the bride stopped in the next day, it was in pieces on the floor – she had pulled the whole thing apart to start over. At that point, the bride decided to cut her losses and walk away. (This is when they called me in a panic that they had less than a week to find a gown that fit. Thankfully I had a great shop I referred her to and all was well in her world.)

## Trying on gowns – appointments required

- Many shops you walk into won't let you come in off the street and start trying on wedding gowns. I have several theories about this. They will tell you that an appointment is required, they don't have a fitter available or any number of other reasons. They'll also make you register.

Here's what I think about these items:

• Appointments required – I think that because, as women, we feed off each other. We get hyped around other girls. We'll squeal about this gown or that dress because we're giddy little girls playing dress up. I think bridal shops schedule appointments in clusters to create that hype. It sells more dresses.

• Fitters available – they're really the deal closers. The guy at the car dealership that comes in at the end and makes everyone just a little uncomfortable. They pin the dress, too and put the $500 veil on your head and start the gushing.

• Registration required – Two words. Mailing list. For eternity. Cite "witness protection program" and use an alias.

Once again, I'm not bashing retail bridal clothing establishments. It's a tough business. And because I'm a small business owner, I will always push people to the mom-and-pop shops. The examples I illustrated above were "big box" bridal shops. Their employees will be paid whether or not they sell a single dress. If the little guy doesn't give you good customer service and sell a gown – their kids don't eat. It's really quite simple.

So, know what you're getting into. And bring back-up.

# $99 wedding dresses – you may get what you pay for

It's happened twice. The first one I thought was a fluke. The bride called me into her dressing room to tell me her zipper had come unzipped. Upon closer inspection, I noticed that her zipper had come out completely. The dress fit well, but was not too tight – but I thought perhaps she had strained it somehow by trying it on several times or something that would've caused wear.

With only moments to spare before the opening chord of "Here Comes the Bride", I quickly produced some white thread and a long needle to sew her back into her dress. Thankfully she didn't have any reason to need her zipper for the remainder of the evening. I had to give her groom instruction on how to get her out of it. (His choices were scissors or rip the threads – I never asked which method prevailed, although I have a sneaking suspicion.)

The second time it happened was a very thin bride who was losing the shoulder stitching on a tank dress (not typically a high-stress area of clothing construction). We discovered it as she was getting ready to walk down the aisle. I suggested that she not breathe until she came back down the aisle and we would take care of it then. Apparently she breathed, because when she got back to me – they were barely holding on.

Once again, I came armed with my white thread and needle

and took to stitching her back into her dress. There are several wedding pictures with me in them sewing her back in.

My first theory was that the manufacturer used a special thread that dissolved when heated up to body temperature, but that didn't make much sense. So, the only thing I can come up with is you just may get what you pay for. As great as the $99 rack looks when planning a wedding on a budget – keep looking. It may cause more grief that it's worth.

# Save the glass slippers for Cinderella

Let me paint the picture… spring day, birds chirping, flowers blooming, gazebo decorated, guests seated, music playing… Can you see it?

Our venue has a set of tall French doors through which our brides and their bridesmaids enter the garden. They lead onto a landing with steps to get them onto the winding brick sidewalk. Because of these steps, we typically station the appropriate groomsmen at the bottom of the stairs to help the bridesmaids down them. It ends up looking very chivalrous and cute in pictures.

My stupid joke that I tell the groomsmen at the rehearsal that it is their job is to keep the girls from hitting the bricks. If they start to go – it's their job to come between the bridesmaid and the sidewalk.

Here's the second part of the set-up... acrylic shoes with a 6" heel. It's bad news no matter how you slice it. To complicate the matter – let's add a long dress on a heavy bridesmaid.

Recipe for disaster? Oh, yeah.

As I'm standing at the door telling the bridesmaids when to go, this bridesmaid says to me, "What if I fall?"

I said, "Sister, it's never happened before. I'm not starting with you." Then I tapped her on the arm signifying it was time for her to go.

She did everything she was supposed to do. She gracefully walked across the deck. She reached for the outstretched hand of her groomsman. She took the first step. Then the second step. Then something went horribly wrong... from my vantage point – all I saw was a big shiny bridesmaid dress fly up in the air. (Side note – the groomsman didn't come between her and the sidewalk.)

She had not compensated for the extremely high heel and a bad knee. When she stepped off the last step and onto the sidewalk, she hadn't factored in that her heel was as high as it was. Bad knee. Bad shoes. Bad things happen.

She bounced off her bad knee, got dragged back to her feet by her groomsman, and made it down the aisle with blood running down her leg.

Moral of the story – don't try to walk in shoes you can't walk in, especially when people are watching and there is a photographer poised and ready. Sometimes it doesn't end well.

# Just because they own cameras doesn't make them photographers

"My friend has a really nice camera." I hear this a lot. Here's what I will offer – I have a really nice stove. That doesn't make me a chef.

There are any number of things that can go wrong when you don't hire a professional:

- No good photos – this was more of a problem when film was the photo medium. A photographer couldn't tell immediately if they had gotten the shot or not. Or if the film had been over- or under-exposed. They could also have issues when developing film that would render it completely useless. Early on, I had brides who came to me later and said they had not a single photo from their wedding day. To me, this would be devastating.

- No eye for the obvious – I always suggest that brides ask a photographer for an album of a full wedding, not carefully selected photos in a portfolio. Was the photographer strong in the beginning, but weak at the end? If this was your wedding album – would you be happy with it? I also suggest covering up the bride's face (we're emotionally attached to her) and look at everything else. Is everyone's head in the photo? Their faces? How about the guys on the end? Do we have hands with no heads? How about trash cans? Are they in the shot, too?

- No eye for the technical – There are so many fancy knobs, buttons and settings on a professional's camera. The difference is they know how to use them all to their advantage. With today's electronics, we have really great cameras in our pockets in the form of cell phones, but no extra knobs (filters don't count).

- No organization skills – it takes a lot to organize, collect and shoot a large number of people in a short amount of time. Most professional photographers will ask their couples a thousand questions before the day, so as to make sure they get everything required of them. A photographer needs to be direct, but not abrasive to get photos lined up, shot and the bridal party back to the reception quickly.

- No editing skills – have you ever seen the acronym "WYSIWYG"? It means, what you see is what you get. I've seen photographers edit some very unsightly things out of a wedding photo – to include an inappropriate saying on a t-shirt (yes, some people actually wear t-shirts with inappropriate sayings on them to weddings). Without a professional and their editing skills – what you see is what you get.

- Printing capability – with today's digital world, many of our photos never make it out of our digital devices. It's sad, really. Hopefully, there will be at least one "oh wow" photo that you want printed for your home. Professional photographers work with the best labs with the best equipment to make sure you get an heirloom quality print. Most online labs or corner stores can't offer that. Once your wedding photo fades to white – what do you have left?

One final word on photographers and wedding photos – besides your new spouse, your photos are really all you take away from the wedding day with you. If you need to skimp on something, let it be something else. When planning my own wedding, I took a survey of friends and co-workers on what they wished they would've spent more money on at their wedding. Without being prompted, every single person responded – "photographer". So, there you have it. Spend less on the alcohol and appetizers – more on the photographer.

# Whoever said disposable cameras on the tables are a good idea?

We've all seen it, right? The disposable camera on the table? Typically there's a card or something that invites you to take photos of yourself and the others at your table. It's meant to be a fun way of capturing candid shots and making the guests interact with each other.

Have you ever thought about how that will ACTUALLY work? There's usually one (sometimes two) per table. They usually have 27 exposures. So, let's say you have 100 guests. Figuring tables that seat 8 – we're looking at approximately 13 tables. At one camera per table – you're talking about 351 pictures. And by pictures, I mean tangible photos printed on photo paper (that you have to take to a photo shop, etc. to develop). If you put TWO on each table, you're looking at over 700 photos.

I just Googled pricing at Walgreen's for development pricing – it runs about $12 per camera. Price wise (not counting the price of the camera – usually around $6/each) – you're looking at $156 just to develop the film. (So cameras + developing = approximately $234.) Doesn't sound terrible, right? Under $250 for a fun activity that everyone suggests and seems to love! Let's order some cute cameras and get started!

Please consider these points:

• Children love these. A lot. I've seen 27 pictures of a child's left ear. Seriously. Sometimes they look through the wrong side and click pictures. They are also fascinated by their feet. They will photograph them in 27 different locations. They think they're all different pictures.

• Drunks like them, too. One should not be surprised by inappropriate photos of nether regions. Or cleavage. Lots of it.

• Grandma wants everything to be just how you wanted it. So she'll participate, too. Trouble is, she can't really see through that tiny little view finder – so she'll just click the button. Important things normally get left out – like people's heads.

• Your well-meaning friends will all lean in for a photo at the table. That will eat up one or two per roll. Maybe someone will finish the roll. Maybe not. The film development price is still the same.

So -- before you consider the disposable camera, ask yourself this: Do I want 702 photos of ears, feet and cleavage? If no, skip it and try something else.

I think you'll be glad you did.

# Just because the venue allows self-catering doesn't mean you should do it

Oh, where to start with this one. There are so many ways this can go horribly wrong.

Time: There's never enough of it. I had a bride and groom that were insistent on doing everything themselves. The groom had a perfect vision of how the food would look, taste and be presented. What he hadn't counted on was how long it would take to make food for 100 guests. He ended up being horribly late getting to the venue, then had very specific ways that he wanted the food to be plated. The plating itself was labor intensive and too many hands on deck turned it into a confusing mess. He nearly missed his own wedding because of the mayhem in the kitchen. As it was, we started nearly two hours late.

Workload: The thing about preparing food for a large amount of people, is that it's a large amount of food. And most residential kitchens are not equipped to handle large amounts of food for extended periods of time. We had an event where the women in the family all got together to prepare a Mexican food feast. There were roasters full of shredded beef and large pots of pinto beans. The cheese, lettuce, etc. was all prepackaged, so it was fine. The problem was with storing the food overnight. They opted to turn the heat off and let it sit out overnight. In the late afternoon, they turned the heat back on. By the time dinner was served, portions of the meat and beans had spoiled. Her entire party ended up being sick all weekend.

Logistics: How do we get it to the venue? It's a tough question. I have had large roasters and crock pots delivered in large Rubbermaid tubs packed in beach towels. I've had myriad food items delivered after being dumped directly into plastic grocery bags. I've had salad dressing arrive in Ziploc bags. Not to mention potato salad/coleslaw/etc. packed into plastic shoeboxes. None of which are approved food handling methods.

Quantity: How much do we make? Depending on the menu and the culture of the family – this question can be answered a thousand different ways. I had one grandmother tell me that she plans on 1 pound of meat per person. A pound of meat? That's a LOT of meat. Imagine what 100 pounds of meat looks like in a Rubbermaid tote. What typically happens is that we have WAY TOO MUCH food, or it falls very short. They seldom, if ever, come close to being right.

When you hire a caterer, they can address all of these points.

- **Time** – they have it. It's what they do. You stick to getting ready and posing for photos.

- **Workload** – they have the equipment to properly handle large amounts of food. And can cook and store it at safe temperatures.

- **Logistics** – they're in the business. They have the appropriate transportation methods and carriers for food items.

- **Quantity** – they have formulas they use to determine how much food they need. They seldom, if ever, get it wrong.

- **Considering** what you spend in time, containers and wasted food – you probably could have hired a caterer. It's not a luxury. It's a necessity.

# Pizza and ice cream are not reception foods

The bride and groom were young – probably early twenties. They were getting married at their church, but having their reception at my venue. We talked a lot about colors, decorations, layout, etc. The bride's mother had a lot of ideas. The bride didn't like any of them. Or many of them.

They were on a pretty tight budget and trying to get things done for as little as possible. When we got to the food portion of the conversation, it was a tough discussion. Food tends to be one of the most expensive choices of the event. We talked about a dessert buffet. We talked about appetizers only. We talked about Italian and pasta – inexpensive, but feeds a lot of people. The bride didn't like any of the options. She decided that she wanted to talk it over with the groom and would let me know.

She called me back a day or so later and told me that they had finally decided on their menu. Pizza and ice cream. Their favorite foods.

Uh, pizza and ice cream? For 150 guests? In Arizona? At the end of summer? I jumped into action and called my vendors to see the best way to get this done. They all told me the same thing – they would do their best, but logistically – it was nearly impossible. Pizza gets soggy. Ice cream melts. And there's no good way to serve either without a lot of equipment and people. The bride was not happy that she could not be accommodated.

So, back to the drawing board she went. As long stories go, I'll shorten it. They ended up with muffins, cupcakes and wedding cake. They saved the pizza and ice cream for another day.

# DIY often spells D-I-S-A-S-T-E-R

Cake. How hard can it be? Flour, eggs, water and frosting – right? Unless you're a pastry chef, an engineer or an architect – this is not a place to cut corners or think you can do it yourself.

I have had more than one occasion where the bride and/or

her family or well-meaning friend baked the wedding cake. In theory it sounds like a relatively easy task – everyone has baked a cake, cupcakes or cookies in their lifetime. But let me tell you, wedding cakes are a whole different animal.

I have cut into cakes of amateurs who thought they were doing the bride a favor and found a spectrum of sins – ranging from using frosting to mask holes and gaps, to stuffing plastic bags into the voids then frosting over them. Not to mention the use of wooden pencils and plastic knives to stack the cake.

A well-baked and well-built wedding cake can stand alone. It has been baked with a consistency that allows a little bit of weight to be placed on it (i.e., cake topper) and has been built to withstand the weight of itself (stacked cake with columns, etc.).

We haven't even talked about cake flavors and fillings yet. Pastry chefs know (through their training) what you can fill a cake with and what never works. Betty Crocker's intent was never for the mixes to be used for a wedding cake. And Smucker's didn't make strawberry jelly to be used as cake filling. These two things together are a recipe for a disaster. A boxed cake mix doesn't hold together well and strawberry jelly cake filling turns into a drippy, runny mess that causes the cake layers to slip off each other.

There is also engineering and architecture that goes into a wedding cake. Although it may look like the cake is stacked on itself – it truly is not. There are very specific plates, spacers and columns used to make sure your cake stays where it should.

Also, many DIY bakers don't realize that those cute little pearls used by professionals to dot the cake are actually edible. I have picked many plastic pearls off a cake before I served it to guests.

Do yourself a favor – shop around, taste lots of cakes and thank your friend/aunt/mother/neighbor very politely and say "no, thank you" when they offer to bake your wedding cake. Remember – it's an important "Kodak moment" accessory and it needs to look great. And it's the last thing your guests will eat at your reception. Don't leave a bad taste in their mouths.

# Rules were made to be broken. Contracts weren't.

We've all heard the phrase "rules were made to be broken". I'm not sure exactly how true that is, but as humans, we definitely push the envelope. We drive a little too fast. We stand a little too close. And twenty items in the fast lane doesn't REALLY mean twenty items, right?

Contracts are another thing altogether. We expect protection with contracts -- whether we're buying a house, buying a car or booking a venue for a special occasion. In all the years I've been in business, this has only been tested twice. And by tested, I mean argued.

My contract is very basic and simple without any fine print. It says what the renter can expect from us (the venue) and what we expect out of them (payments). It's spelled out very clearly that deposits and payments are non-refundable. In fact, it says it after every payment/dollar amount that is listed. It's not buried in another paragraph, on the next page or hidden anywhere else. It's right there. In plain sight.

It doesn't happen often, but it does happen. I've been accused of only protecting myself and being out to get my customers. I can assure you that is definitely not the case.

Here's how it works. We sign a contract. We lock in the date, time and expectations. I agree to it. You agree to it. Both of our signatures indicate that agreement. We're all set. This means that I can't bump a customer for a better offer, a bigger party or more money. Period. This also means that the customer is locked in, as well. It's not a trick. It's not a tactic. It's considered good business.

I had a bride who had booked our venue more than a year in advance of her wedding date. She and her father diligently and faithfully paid down her balance. We were kind and pleasant to each other. I accommodated multiple meetings, phone calls and questions – like I do with all of my brides. Then one day she called and demanded a full refund. They were no longer in need of our services.

I kindly explained that our contract states "non-refundable" and that I would gladly move her payments and deposits to another date. Nope. Full refund. At which time, I reminded her of the non-refundable contract. She indicated that she and the groom had been working with a choreographer for their first dance and that our dance floor couldn't accommodate the dance. Therefore, a full refund was necessary. (Side note: no changes had been made to the venue since the contract was signed.)

Final word on contracts: know what you're signing. Keep a copy. Realize that although it may look like your needs aren't being protected – they actually are.

# When you hire the DJ – keep in mind your grandmother will be in attendance

"Know your audience." Words to live by. And words to share with your disc jockey.

We had the wedding and reception of a couple that came from a very strict religious background. Their families, as it turned out, were also very strict with their religion. There were several things that have become somewhat "normal" in today's culture, which will never be accepted in certain religious cultures – i.e., living together, premarital sex, etc. One should be extremely careful when assuming what is acceptable and appropriate in each family.

The DJ seemed to be holding his own. Music was playing,

people were dancing, it appeared that a good time was being had by all. Then he grabbed the microphone and asked all of the girls who were holding keys to come to the dance floor (he had handed keys to several single girls prior to this request and told them he would call them up later). He went into a big charade about all of the single girls' hearts that were breaking and they all needed to return his apartment keys – he was off the market now; a married man.

(Insert the sound of crickets…)

The "joke" was totally lost on this crowd. Their religious culture was very specific as to no premarital anything. Offspring lived with their parents until they were married. Couples entered into their marriage covenants pure. (Novel idea – I know, but truly it still exists.)

So, back to the DJ. Instead of realizing that he had blown this particular joke and moving on, he made a meager attempt at explaining the joke. (Insert the sound of more crickets…) I ran to his aid and suggested that he keep the music on and the microphone off. It was the awkward moment of all awkward moments and the bride's face was red the entire evening. She was concerned what her grandmother had thought of her.

Still on the topic of DJs, but on to different events. Be aware that your grandmother (mother, aunt, church lady) will be in attendance. Just because you downloaded the explicit version of your favorite song on your iPod does not make it appropriate for public consumption. I've been placed in the difficult position several times when the grandmother (mother, aunt, church lady) leaned over me saying, "WHAT did he just say?"

Some lyrics are rated MA (mature audience). Even some of our most mature guests don't appreciate the art of some music. Please play accordingly.

My response when they ask? "Oh, I'm not sure. I don't listen to this stuff."

Even if it's downloaded on my own iPod.

# Limos and their drivers

During my twenty years in business, I have met several really great limousine drivers from some really great companies. My first experience was with a small business owner with one limo and he was the driver. It was a terrific experience every single time. Unfortunately, he ended up moving across the country and there have been many years of struggles since then.

One such time was a limousine driver who couldn't figure out where she was. It was nearing the end of the event and I had called to make sure the driver would be onsite at the designated time. She assured me she was already onsite. To which I responded, no she wasn't, as I was onsite and did not see her. She described the building she was sitting in front of. I described the building I was standing in front of – complete with the address and a large sign proclaiming the name of my venue.

Instead of realizing that she wasn't where she needed to be, she continued to argue with me that she was where she was supposed to be. It seemed that no amount of reasoning with her could sway her into realizing that she wasn't at the venue. When I pushed her on why she was so adamant that she was in the right place (when clearly she wasn't) – she said that's where her navigation had sent her, therefore, she was in the right place.

Realizing that I was getting absolutely nowhere with her because I could see her at the end of the street, I sent an employee to retrieve her and bring her to the venue. I'm not sure exactly what he said to her, but it took him awhile to convince her that the bride wasn't coming out of the small house she was sitting in front of.

Another situation we encountered with a limo driver wasn't about a navigation system, but his perceived schedule. The driver had been a bit overscheduled. He had dropped off our bridal party, then had been sent to pick up and deliver another party (not sure the nature of the second party). He arrived at the venue before his scheduled time – probably by about 30 minutes early. He came to the gate and spoke to the security guard so we knew he was onsite – which sometimes happens. Only he wasn't just letting us know he was here. His message was (and I quote), "If they're not in the limo in ten minutes – I'm leaving without them."

When my employee alerted me to the situation, I seriously thought he was kidding. So, I decided to go speak to the driver myself. At which time, he told me that if this bridal party wasn't in the limo in the next ten minutes, he was leaving without them.

I went back into the party to locate my bride and let her know of the "situation". But in the meantime, I sent another employee over to chit-chat with the driver. I sent a bottle of water and a piece of wedding cake. My employee chatted with him about his job. Does he meet nice people? What's the strangest party he's driven around? Does it pay well? Pretty much anything he could come up with to stall him and not let him leave.

So, long story short – he didn't leave without the bride or her party. Perhaps those are some questions that should be asked when booking a limo service. Will he ACTUALLY leave us? If so, it would've certainly ended a GREAT night on a bad note – for no legitimate reason.

Two points to remember:

- Hire a limo driver that can read a map or follow a GPS system

- "If you're not in the car by 10 p.m., I'm leaving without you" is not considered good customer service

# There's a reason minors aren't allowed to drink alcohol

I believe that most states have liquor laws. More specifically, drinking ages. In Arizona, it's not just a suggestion – it's the law. You must be twenty-one.

Because I own/operate a private event venue, some people make the assumption that I'm not paying attention. Or that because it's a private party or an "open bar", that those laws aren't closely monitored.

I've had teenaged kids come up to the bar and say, "My mom said I could have a beer." Um… no.

There have been several occasions where I found discarded liquor bottles under the tables after the party was over – liquor that wasn't served from the bar or bartender. Usually, these are the adults wanting hard liquor, when we only allow beer and wine.

There is one particular event that I remember very clearly. The teenage girl came to the bar and asked for a beer (her mom said she could – see above). The bartender refused to serve her. Then the mother came to the bar and told the bartender she said her daughter could have a beer. The bartender still refused. The mother then decided that she would get her own drinks, and then give them to her daughter out of our sight.

We clued in pretty quickly as to what was going on, then the mother was also refused service. It became quite comical watching the mother and her daughter trying to put others up to coming to the bar to collect drinks for both of them. Because we were now monitoring them and everyone they spoke to, they were unable to be served any more alcohol. This wedding reception became very boring to them and they decided to leave.

A considerable time later – probably about an hour – someone came in looking for me. I followed them outside to see a fight in the parking lot. The mother and daughter were tearing into each other with the fervor of angry feral cats. Hair, shoes and skimpy dresses were flying. It wasn't pretty. I have absolutely no idea what the fight was about, but I'm fairly sure the alcohol on board didn't help the situation, at all.

I'm not sure that twenty-one would have made much of a difference, but it certainly couldn't have hurt anything.

# Party favors are not a competitive sport

Party favors. Who knows exactly where the concept came from? I've read that it came from English aristocracy as a way to show their infinite wealth and royalty. I've also read that brides would send home small pieces of their wedding cake with single women so they could sleep on them and dream of their future grooms. There are probably several other variations of how the tradition started, but however it did – we all love them.

In my years as the owner of a wedding venue, I have seen many trends come and go in the party favor arena. We've seen literal tons of Hershey's kisses bundled in tulle circles tied up with wedding-color-appropriate ribbon and seed packets with the couple's names emblazoned on them. There are any number of little bags, boxes, tins, shot glasses, etc. that can hold anything from Jordan almonds to butter mints to the bride's favorite peanut butter cup.

At some point along the way – and I can't pin a specific date to it – it's like party favors became a competitive sport. Our Hershey kiss bundles made way to crystal wine bottle stoppers, bottle openers shaped like stilettos and stained glass candle holders etched with the couple's names and wedding date.

Beautiful? Absolutely. Practical? Probably not.

Here are a few things to consider:

- As fabulous as these items are -- nobody REALLY wants an (insert bauble name here) with YOUR name and wedding date on it. Really. If you want to provide these items – skip the etching and let it just be a gift.

- Anything not food related (candy, cookies, etc.) invariably gets re-packed at the end of the event and sent home with the bride.

- After the hum and buzz of your blissful wedding day have passed – what are YOU going to do with an extra case of crystal wine stoppers with last week's date on them?

There is no wrong or right way to tackle the question of party favors. We do truly love them. It's nice to come away from any party with a little token. Just be smart about it. Think ALL the way through it. The best piece of advice my mother gave me about my own wedding? It's the biggest day in YOUR life, not theirs. Plan accordingly.

# Just because you live in Arizona doesn't mean it won't rain on your wedding day

Arizona is known for its 350 plus sunny days a year. It almost NEVER rains. This particular year, it hadn't rained for months. All the news weather forecasters were losing their minds. Every single day they were sure to tell us that it had been X-amount of days since our last measurable rainfall.

Then they started telling us about an impending storm. A storm of the century. One that couldn't be avoided. The weather wonks said there was 100 percent chance of rain. That's right -- ONE HUNDRED PERCENT chance of rain.

As I always did, I contacted my bride two days prior to the wedding to ask her if she wanted me to rent a tent. I had a standing "hold" on a large tent at a rental company, but because of the 100 percent chance of rain, they were pushing me to reserve it, or let it go. My bride opted to let it go. She let it go.

*Vendors*

On Friday, before her wedding on Saturday, the storm was blowing in. It was big and it was packing a bunch of rain. I called her and offered to reschedule her wedding to Sunday. There was 0 percent chance of rain that day. I would contact her vendors and help her contact her guests. No, thank you. She REALLY wanted this particular date.

So, her date came. And so did the rain. A lot of it. Torrential amounts of it. She managed to scrape together enough EZ-UP tents to keep most people somewhat dry. It was a wet, soggy mess. The bridesmaids went down the aisle with red umbrellas. The bride went with a white one. (It was actually quite cute.)

We made it through the wedding and were ready to start the reception. Typically what happens at this time, is we take care of the paperwork – we sign the marriage license. When I asked her for it, I got a blank stare. A marriage license? I asked her if she had forgotten it at home. No. She had never purchased one.

So after all of that, she ended up not really getting married that day. We met up again after the honeymoon and made it official.

It was sunny and beautiful on Sunday.

# Wedding location – reception at home

Many people come to me and say they're just looking for a place for their ceremony and they're planning their reception at home. To some, this sounds like a logical option – the wedding ceremony is the "important" part. The reception is just a party. Right?

Partially.

The ceremony IS the most important part of that day. And logistically, it's the easiest part. There are very few "moving parts" to the wedding ceremony itself. The long and short of it is chairs, decorations, music and an officiant. It's also the legal part. Let's not screw that part up.

But the reception is where things get complicated. The logistics get a little more complex. Here are some points to ponder:

**The space:**
- What does your backyard look like?
- Will it need an entire overhaul? New landscaping?
- Entrance? Is there a gate? Will people have to come through the house?
- Is your living room large enough to accommodate a party in case of inclement weather?
- Is there a pool? Rocks?
- Do you have dogs?

## Restrooms:

- Where are they?
- Are you going to need to rent a port-a-potty or two? Where does that go? Is there a hand washing station?
- If no porta-pottys, do you want people in your house using yours? What if it backs up?

## Rentals – tables, chairs, linens and china:

- What is the cost to rent them?
- Where do I rent them from?
- Is there a place to park the rental truck for loading and unloading?
- What do I have to do with the rentals once I'm done?
- Do they need to be stacked a certain way in a specific area?
- How do the soiled linens need to be handled?
- How do I return dirty dishes?
- Why is the pick up so inconvenient?

## Vendors:

- Who will be there to let them in?
- Do they have ample room to set their stations up?
- Is the kitchen large enough to accommodate a catering staff?
- Are you even using vendors? If you're self-catering, who is taking care of kitchen logistics, food, timing and handling?

## Trash:

- Who is picking it up off the tables?
- What are you doing with it?
- Will your residential garbage cans accommodate that amount? If not, what?
- Who bought the large trash bags?
- Do we have enough cans to set around?

## Parking:

- Where are your guests going to park?
- Is there enough room in the neighborhood?
- How far will your guests have to walk?
- What if the neighbors are throwing a party the same night?

## Permits:

- Some cities require permits for events like these. Be sure to check with your local jurisdiction.

## Noise Ordinances:

- Look them up in your area. Ask questions.
- These are typically by complaint only and monitored by local police departments
- Neighbors don't like noise.

## General Logistics:

- Have you done this before?
- Will you be able to enjoy yourself during the event?
- Who is in charge?
- Who deals with crisis or unforeseen challenges?
- Who is going to clean it up?

The logistics of a large, albeit very important, party are very different – even if you just want "something casual". Once you redo the landscaping, rent all of the furniture and equipment, and break your back setting it up and cleaning it up – you may have been better off renting a venue. Not to mention having the carpet shampooed when it's over, or having to redo the bathroom because the toilet backed up. It's worth shopping around. Then letting someone else worry about the trash, toilets and soiled linens. You'll probably be glad you did.

# Spray tans – color on the run

A wedding day is a big deal. We all want to look our best. We want all of the sparkle and glow we can get. We spend a lot of time worrying about our dress, our hair, our jewelry, our weight – everything needs to be tip-top. What we often realize (especially us pale girls) is that a pale girl in a white dress isn't the look we want. So, we should work on our skin tone, right?

We all PLAN to spend some extra time in the sun getting just the right glow. As with most things, time ticks by. Projects take longer than we expect. We end up not having time to build a slow, good, tan base. In our friends' infinite wisdom, they offer sound, sage advice about just getting a spray tan. Bingo! Problem solved.

Here's where the plot changes. The story I want to share with you was actually the GROOM'S tale of woe. He was a very handsome, blonde, buff guy. He was marrying an incredibly beautiful Latina. He wanted to surprise her with a golden glow.

It was a little warm that day. The wedding was a brunch/ lunchtime affair. The groom was wearing a white tux. They were dancing and having the time of their lives. It got a little warm, so the groom removed his tux coat. I stared at him for a good long time trying to figure out what I was seeing. I couldn't really figure it out. As I got a closer look, I realized he was sweating orange.

I quickly pulled him aside and pointed it out to him. He

97

howled with laughter and told me had had gotten a spray tan earlier that day as a surprise for his new bride. What he didn't realize was that he should've gotten it a day or two earlier and showered at least once. Let me tell you, she was surprised!

Lesson: Make sure you ask a lot of questions and know what the rules are before you get a spray tan, wear white and sweat.

# I'm 70 years old – Explain It To Me

She was one of my favorite moms. We talked a lot during the planning of her son's wedding. She was doing a really good job respecting the bride's wishes and her space while they waltzed through the planning process. They were choreographing who was paying for what, what would be eliminated because of price and what mom was willing to add back in and pay for.

At one point, the exasperated mom said, "I'm 70 years old; please explain it to me!" As it turns out, there are a lot of not-so-traditional wedding traditions. Here are a few:

**Bridal party:** Brides don't always follow the traditions of bridesmaids. Sometimes they have bridesmen. It happens. As we grow up, we have friends – sometimes even boys that are best friends. It seems unfair that they wouldn't get a prime spot next to the bride. Conversely, we also have best maids/groomsmaids – same reason.

**Cake toppers:** Gone are the plastic versions of blonde brides and brunette grooms in awkward poses. Brides (and grooms) are using the tops of their cakes to express themselves and their individuality. I've seen everything from clowns to skateboards to spiders on cakes. They now have lots of choices in this department. And they're fun. They're just not traditional.

**Who pays for what?:** Traditionally, the bride's family paid for the wedding. The groom's family paid for the rehearsal dinner. But now, brides and grooms are paying for much of these expenses on their own. And traditionally, whoever was paying for it had the bigger voice in the decision-making process. So that sometimes ends up clouding the water. As well as the guest list. Just play nice and figure it out. Together.

**Gowns:** White traditionally meant purity. Ivory meant not. Now it means what color you look best in. And some brides wear red. Or black. It's no reflection on their past lives or revelations of sin. They just like red.

**Kids in the bridal party:** Not just any kids – the bride's kids. Or the groom's kids. More than ever, today's families are non-traditional. Nobody "has" to get married anymore. We marry because we choose to, not because we are forced. And divorce is much more common now than ever, and with that comes a variety of family blending.

**"Giving Away" the bride:** Actually now, we use the word "escort" – who is escorting the bride down the aisle? There are multiple variations of this. Brides are more apt to choose someone who held a role of great importance in their lives as their aisle escort – and it's not always their fathers. Many brides don't have fathers, or relationships with their fathers. Many are closer to their stepdads than their biological dads. Some brides have older sons/daughters that they raised as single parents – they got through lots together, let's do this, too. And other brides feel like they have no one, so we send the groom back up the aisle to get her. No matter how it gets done, we'll get the bride delivered to her groom and the officiant.

**Catering:** Gone are the days of chicken breast and rice pilaf. Food is another way brides express their personalities. Anything goes – from street tacos to food trucks – nothing should surprise you. And let's not forget the many different ways that people eat – gluten-free, vegan, vegetarian, etc.

**Wedding cake:** Not everyone likes cake – or so I hear. We've had brides serve pie, cupcakes, cheesecake or just a huge dessert assortment.

It would seem that the only thing traditional about marriage is the word "marriage". Roll with it. Love is love – no matter what they are wearing, who is standing next to them or what they serve for dinner.

# Angels Among Us

## Unexplained Occurrences

When we first purchased Virginia's House, it had been a long time since any renovations had been done on the home. Based on the wall color, carpet and linoleum – a fair guess would be the 1960s.

Almost immediately we started painting, removing layers of wallpaper, carpet, stripping paint, etc. We spent every available moment doing something to the house.

Because we were working on several rooms at a time, we slept wherever we weren't working at the time. At one point, our bed was in the very front room (currently the bride's dressing room).  One night, we were sound asleep when the something woke us up. At first, it was one of those did-I-really-hear-that situations.  Then it happened again, but much louder this time.

It sounded like someone had thrown handfuls of pea gravel at the windows.  We immediately jumped up to see if anyone was out there.  There wasn't a single thing moving on the street.  As we sat there talking about what we had heard, we both agreed that we heard rocks hit two different sides of the house at the same time – something that would've been impossible with the location of a block fence.

When the sun came up we went outside to assess what it was – fully expecting to see small rocks or even eggs.  Nothing. There was absolutely nothing out there.

On another occasion, we had moved our bed to yet another room.  Because we didn't have air conditioning on the house, we all piled into one room that had a window unit to sleep. During the night, my husband heard an old time, crank phone ringing.  He sat up to see where it was coming from and the dog was already at full alert.  I didn't hear this one, but he swears it happened.

When I was still working my corporate job, I got a call from the alarm company that there was a glass break sensor activation, followed by a motion detection in the hallway.  The police had shown up and found nothing.  When we got home, we looked everywhere for something out of place or something that possibly could've fallen and set off the glass break sensor. We looked literally everywhere, including the upstairs apartment that was blocked off from the rest of the building. Nothing.

We were outside on our back porch when the neighbor yelled over the wall, "Hey, is everything okay over there? I heard glass breaking this afternoon. I just wanted to check on you guys." We still have no idea what it was.

I was sitting with a bride at the desk where we do contracts in the room that was the home's original dining room. We were chatting while I wrote her contract. I had my left hand palm up while I was writing with my right hand. A small bent nail landed in my hand. I looked at her, we both looked up at the ceiling (there was nowhere it could've fallen from up there), I looked back at her and asked if she still wanted to sign the contract. She said yes, but she wanted the nail. I gave it to her.

On another occasion, I was sitting with a bride, her mom and her aunt. The mom and her sister wanted to know if the house was "haunted", so I was telling them the stories written above. The bride was saying that she didn't believe that stuff when a gold Christmas ball rolled out from under the desk. It was summertime – no reason there would be a lagging Christmas ornament in there. The bride bolted out the door, then came back in and tried to get me to tell her that she had been set-up. She hadn't been.

# Female angels

Just like her male counterpart, we have a female angel or ghost. She happens to reside in our guest house. She did not make herself known for quite some time.

In fact, we truly didn't even realize that she existed until we had to tear down and rebuild the guest house to accommodate my business for handicapped access. We were having a hard time keeping electrical contractors. They would work for a day or so, then never return.

I asked an intuitive friend of mine what she thought the issue was. She said that Grace (our apparition's name) didn't fully understand the concept of electricity, so she was unintentionally blocking their progress. She indicated that I should go out there and tell her I needed her to stop doing that. Of course, I had no idea what that even meant! She suggested that I take the dog outside with me, watch where the dog went (she would be drawn to the energy), then talk to that spot.

So…one night I took the dog out to the framed-out building and watched her. She went directly to the corner and wagged her tail. So I followed her and started talking. I told her that I was trying very hard to finish her (Grace's) new house and that I needed her to understand that things are different now. If she wouldn't mind, I needed help getting things done. (Of course, this whole time I worried about my husband coming out there, hearing me and having me locked up in padded room.) After that, we had no more issues and we got things done quickly.

After the house was completed, we were working an event. Our trees are wrapped in white lights and one tree had a string out. One of my employees went out and replaced the string, but still couldn't get it to work. I asked if she had addressed Grace. At which time she said, "Grace, please!" A few minutes later, the tree fully lit up. We haven't had to change a string on it since.

Grace is also a bit competitive with our brides. I have a certain song that I play when our brides go down the aisle. My stereo would shut itself off at the same point in the song every single time. I tried everything from getting a new recording of the song, a new CD, a new file on my electronic device, etc. Then I really started paying attention to when it was happening – it wasn't a certain spot in the song, it was when the bride got to a certain spot on the aisle – the spot where she came into full view of her guests.

Now, as I'm turning on the bride's song, I ask Grace to just let her have this one. So far, so good.

From what I've been able to piece together about Grace, from the mediums who have shared information with me – Grace was a young bride of an Air Force soldier. They lived on the property at some point in time. She had gone downtown one day and bought "clicky" shoes (girls, you know what I mean – grown up lady shoes that make the "clicky" sound when you walk). She was so excited to show her husband her new shoes when he got home, but he was unhappy that she had spent the money. She was upset by this and left the house crying. She was running and sobbing and ended up running in front of a train that ultimately killed her. Her death was ruled a suicide and she's angry that people would think she would intentionally do that. I haven't been able to find any information about a death that occurred like this, but I've been told pieces of this story by more than one person.

My intuitive friend used to buy jewelry on eBay. She had purchased a lot of rings from one seller and when she received the shipment, there was a locket inside. She contacted the seller and told her that there was a locket in the package that she hadn't paid for. The seller indicated that she only dealt in rings – there was no way the locket came from her.

Upon closer inspection of the locket, the initials "GW" were inscribed on the front. She brought me the locket and told me she thought it belonged to me. When I opened the locket, there was a photo of a young airman inside. I'm pretty sure it belonged to "my" Grace.

# Male angels and other beautiful things

When we first started having events at Virginia's House, several people who claimed to be "intuitive" or "clairvoyant" came in and offered me glimpses of what they "saw" here. At first it was entertaining and I didn't put a lot of merit into what they were saying. They were not anyone I invited in to read the house or anything; they were guests at parties being held here.

But as the years went on, they had the same pull to one area (the butler's pantry) and they all told me variations of the same story. The main house had a semi-angry man who had taken up permanent residence.

Several years ago, we had to call the police for something – honestly, I don't remember what the circumstance was. When the officers got here, they said they had never been to this address before. We told them we were law-abiding and they wouldn't ever spend much time here. One of the officers said, "No. It's different than that. It's almost like a force field here. I've never even looked at this property driving by. I've never actually seen it."

I found that to be bizarre being that we sit on the corner of a major thoroughfare just blocks from the main police station.

As the intuitives kept offering me their feelings about the house, I started asking questions. I wanted to know if my apparition was male or female and what their name was. They all said male and John.

They all indicated that he had previously lived in the home and had regrets for the way he treated his family – so he was hanging around taking care of mine. It was nice to know that we had our very own "house ghost" taking good care of us. Virginia's husband's name was John. We could only assume it is him.

107

That it is him became perfectly clear one afternoon on a spring day. My husband had been at a very long day of work. I had left to pick our daughters up at school. There was a large fire burning south of the valley and at different parts of the day, you could smell smoke in the city.

My husband had come in, taken a shower and fallen asleep on the couch. He said as he was falling asleep that he had a thought that he needed to measure our back porch. He thought it was strange, but then had the thought again so decided he needed to get up right then and do it. (Side note: we had just had that porch slab poured a week or so prior, so neither one of us are sure as to why he thought he needed a measurement.) So, he got up, went outside and measured the porch. As he stepped outside, he noted that he could smell smoke and thought the wind had shifted. He measured and turned to go back inside and noticed that the chandelier on the porch was on fire. We had patio drapes that had frayed on the edges. The wind had blown them up and the threads had wrapped around the base of a light bulb causing it to catch fire. He made quick work of putting the fire out and saving us from a very big and ugly house fire.

The bizarre coincidences told us both that John had been unrelenting in getting him to wake up and get to the back porch. Thankfully he succeeded or our story would've ended there.

John has been very quiet since then, but there's still one ice cold place in the butler's pantry that I've been told is him. We co-habitate just fine with him. And we're glad he's here.

# Butterflies and hummingbirds

Butterflies have long been associated with loved ones that have passed on. Many brides will use them as a way to honor their lost family members. According to Native American legend, if anyone wants a wish to come true, they must first capture a butterfly and whisper the wish to it. Since a butterfly is silent and can make no sound, it can't reveal the wish to anyone but the Great Spirit who sees and hears all, including the silence of the wishing heart. In gratitude for giving the butterfly its freedom, the Great Spirit grants the wish the butterfly has revealed to Him. So according to the legend, by making a wish and setting the butterfly free, the wish is taken to the heavens and granted.

I had a bride who was viewing our venue as a possible site for her upcoming wedding. We were talking about my preferred vendor officiant. I was relaying a story about how she writes each couple's ceremony specifically for them. I used the butterfly reference as an illustration of how she customizes. The bride instantly started tearing up. I told her it was a very sweet ceremony. She said, "No, I asked my dad to let me know if this was the right place. Butterflies were our thing. You would've had no reason to know that, yet you mentioned butterflies."

I was out working in our gardens one day. There was a particularly persistent yellow butterfly that followed me around most of the day. I typically see them out there, but this day it was literally everywhere I looked. Later that day, I had a bride viewing the property. My butterfly friend joined us on the tour. I made mention that he had been following me around all day. She laughed and said, "It's my dad. I sent him in ahead of time." And so she did.

Hummingbirds aren't something that we see that much around here. We see them on occasion, but it's not an every-day occurrence. Again, I was out in the gardens taking care of things. This beautiful hummingbird that was dressed in very shiny blues and greens spent a great deal of time with me. I had a bride come to view the property and we sat outside for awhile enjoying the beautiful weather. My little hummingbird came and hung around the patio furniture with us. The bride asked if the bird came around a lot. I told her no, and that it was strange that he had been here all day. She started to tear up and said she thought it was her dad. They always pointed out hummingbirds to each other. And there he was.

So when I see beautiful butterflies or hummingbirds, I say hi. I'm quite certain they belong to someone who loved them. And I'm glad they come for visits.

*So when I see beautiful butterflies or hummingbirds, I say hi.*

110

# Holes in the floor

Several years ago, I had a very sweet bride who was planning her wedding here. She and her mom spent a lot of time here working through the details and having a great time with the process. One day, the bride's dad stopped in to tell me that the mother had unexpectedly and suddenly died. The bride was having a very hard time with it, but insisted on staying on course and going on with the wedding. So, that's exactly what we did.

The day of the wedding came. Everyone was doing what they were supposed to be doing. The vendors were all here on time and set-up. The bridesmaids and groomsmen were all in check. The bride was happy, but on the verge of tears all day.

About 10 minutes before the ceremony was supposed to start, it started raining. Now I'm a weather nut and I track weather the entire week before event weekends. There was literally nothing in the forecast that would've indicated ANYTHING weather related would cause a set-back. I went outside and looked into the sky – there were LITERALLY no clouds in the sky, but yet, there was rain.

I went into the bride's room and told her that it was raining a bit and that we would wait for it to stop before we proceeded. She very calmly said, "Oh, it's my mother. I'll step outside and tell her to stop."

She grabbed a cigarette and headed out to the front porch.

She was out there for a few minutes. When she came back in, she had been crying, but said things were fine and it had stopped raining.

We dried off the chairs and went on with the ceremony. Her mother had recently won a chair in a raffle – they brought the chair and we set it on the front row for her. The officiant read some very special words about her mother during the ceremony and love was celebrated.

The reception went off without a hitch. Everyone was eating, dancing and having a great time. I heard many people mention how much they missed her and how sad they were that she was missing her daughter's wedding.

When it came time for the first dances, the bride danced with her dad to the country song "Holes in the Floor of Heaven" by Steve Wariner. The song, in part, goes like this:

*Well my little girl is 23,*
*I walk her down the aisle.*
*It's a shame her Mom can't be here now,*
*To see her lovely smile.*
*They throw the rice, I catch her eye,*
*As the rain starts coming down.*
*She takes my hand; says: "Daddy don't be sad,*
*'cause I know Mama's watching now.*
*"'cause there's holes in the floor of Heaven,*
*"And her tears are pouring down.*
*"That's how you know she's watching,*
*"Wishing she could be here now.*
*"An' sometimes if you're lonely,*

*"Just remember she can see.*

*"There's holes in the floor of Heaven"*

During the song, the rain returned. There wasn't a dry eye in the house – including the staff, caterers and bartender. The party was pretty much over at that point.

### 'I knew you would be here'

I had an incredibly wonderful bride several years back. She had told me of the crushing loss of her father and brother in a car accident in recent years. It was still very raw and fresh. I had mentioned that my husband was a police officer and he had seen some pretty horrific things. And I was so very sorry for her losses. I couldn't even imagine.

The day of her wedding, she got here in tears and told me that her mother had been admitted to the hospital very early that morning. She was going to have to get married without any of them here. She was heartbroken.

We made it through the wedding – it was a very small gathering without a reception. They were leaving here and going directly to the hospital to see her mother – wedding clothes and all. They wanted her mother to be included as much as possible.

Later that afternoon, I got a text message from my husband that he had met my bride that day. She was in the bottom car in a horrible five-car pile-up where a car had crossed the center median. My heart stopped. As a man of few words, he said she was fine, but he thought it was weird that she called him by name – especially since he was wearing a reflective traffic vest that would've blocked his name embroidered on his uniform.

I got a phone call from her the next day. Her version of the story was very different. She said when all hell was breaking loose when the accident occurred – she cried out for her dad and brother to protect her. There was a single officer on scene running from car to car seeing what level of injury had occurred. He was standing on top of another car leaning down into hers asking if the occupants were injured.

She yelled back to him, "Are you Officer Stahl?"

He replied, "Yes."

She said, "We're fine. I knew you would be here."

After the smoke had cleared and the tow trucks had removed all of the vehicles from their entanglement, he said that the damage to her vehicle was almost non-existent. He couldn't believe how little damage there was.

She was certain that her father and brother had, in fact, protected her. And that my sweet husband could've been the only one there to dig her out of it.

There are angels among us. Those we can't see. And those in a uniform.

# Conclusion

## Do what you love

Find something you like to do and you'll never work another day in your life. Or some variation of that. Basically, find something you love and do that. And be willing to do that thing and not get paid for it for a while.

That's where it started for me. Except I didn't realize it wouldn't pay me for a while. I thought if I went through the motions – bought the property, placed the magazine ads and listed the phone number – money would show up on my doorstep. That's not exactly how it happened.

Through my years in business, I've come into contact with literally thousands of people. Some people were genuinely interested in what I was doing and wanted to know more about how it all worked. Some people owned their own venues (or wanted to) and got into the business because it looked like "easy money."

Don't get me wrong – we're not splitting the atom here, but there is a lot that goes into making sure parties go off without a hitch. And most of those things were learned the hard way – by doing it wrong. From staffing levels to the amount of toilet paper to have on hand, the minutia adds up.

When I first went into business, I couldn't afford much of a crew – which meant that set-up and clean-up were all on me. My back and feet hurt. A lot. I didn't own my own furniture, so I had to make sure I rented everything I needed, but nothing more – I had to watch every single dime. I lost a lot of sleep wondering if I got enough tables or linens to cover them.

When the bottom dropped out of the economy in 2008, I found myself without a landscaper – mostly because I didn't want to squander the money on that luxury. I spend no less than an hour a day in my gardens making sure things don't get out of hand, but sometimes they still do. It's a never-ending battle that I continue to fight. I've learned the hard way that the landscapers I've tried to hire since then are hellbent to chop everything to dead sticks. So, if I want it done my way, the best way is to do it myself. I plant a lot of flowers. I pull up a lot of dead flowers. It's a never-ending cycle.

I learned the hard way that all people are not nice. Some-times they're downright mean. I had to learn how to stand up for myself without coming across as mean or unprofessional, and without looking or sounding bitchy. Customer service has always been number one to me.

The words I've always lived by are this: Their check cleared the bank. They'll be gone by 10 p.m. That literally got me through events that I thought would never end. When I got to where I could hire staff – those words were repeated to frustrated workers. If nothing else, smile and come get me.

Because I'm a firstborn and a planner, a lot of the necessities were second nature for me. And I quickly learned that efficiency saves both your feet and your back. If I truly looked like I was giving it my best, it's much harder for people to get angry. If I didn't snap at people or look like I was losing my cool, things always went better. Because most people are emotionally charged leading up to the actual ceremony – a smile and a kind word goes a long way. If I could make them laugh – even better.

Organization is the key to most things. I have a system for everything from bride checklists to labeled bins behind the scenes. I stock batteries, band-aids and bottle openers. I keep extra forks, napkins and plastic plates on hand. There's ground coffee in the freezer. I have cake servers and toasting glasses if they forgot theirs. I feel like the Holiday Inn sometimes – if you forgot something, just ask.

The most golden of all my rules is that nobody makes my bride cry. Happy tears are one thing – the other kind, no way.

I've learned to be diplomatic, remove the offender and state the rule clearly. She hired me to take care of things, so take care of things I will. If that means telling your sister to shut up and sit down – so be it. Nicely, of course.

I talk to a lot of vendors and party goers. Many volunteer horror stories of other venues/venue owners. I've heard everything from venue owners refusing to let the florist in because he wasn't done eating his sandwich yet, then sat there and ate it while the flowers sat outside and drooped. Or one that flipped the main power switch at 10 p.m. to indicate that the party was over. It seems like a quick conversation with the DJ would've been sufficient. Or the one that stood inside the building and screamed at the photographer for moving a small table to get a better shot of the bride. It all seems pointless.

I've always wondered why people who don't love people get in the people business. I've always been a helper and a "fixer." If I have the power or the resources, I'll do what I can. I've always lived my life this way. So, this ended up being the perfect fit for me. I can't say I love EVERY minute of it, but I love ALMOST every minute of it. Even when my feet and back hurt.